This book is dedicated
to anyone suffering with
a broken heart.

Six Spiritual Steps to Mend a Broken Heart

Fiona Hickman-Taylor

CYAN

Copyright © 2007 Fiona Hickman-Taylor

First published in 2007 by:

Cyan Communications Limited
119 Wardour Street
London W1F 0UW
United Kingdom
T: +44 (0)20 7565 6120
sales@cyanbooks.com
www.cyanbooks.com

A CIP record for this book is available from the British Library.

ISBN-13 978-1-904879-82-4
ISBN-10 1-904879-82-9

Designed and typeset by Phoenix Photosetting,
Lordswood, Chatham, Kent

Printed and bound in Great Britain by
TJ International Ltd, Padstow, Cornwall

Contents

Acknowledgments

I would like to express my love and gratitude to the following people.

My biggest thank you goes to my darling partner, Ross, who gave me the greatest gift possible—the opportunity of beginning my dream of writing. Without his support this book would never have materialized and for all his love, encouragement, and proofreading I will remain forever grateful.

George, my fantastic son, for being so patient and understanding whenever I had to disappear off to work on the book.

My lovely mother, for all her loving help—in particular her food parcels and babysitting services, both of which were invaluable to the production of this book.

To all my family for their love, support, and positivity, especially Dad and Aunty M.

Acknowledgments

Joyce, my beloved teacher, whose inspiration, wisdom, and love set me on the pathway of light and spiritual unfoldment.

Emma and Tim at Ambo Ltd, for opening up new doorways of possibilities with their inspirational NLP Practitioners course.

Matt at Matt Sills Photography for my fabulous author biography photograph.

Sally, for her lovely friendship, her generosity of spirit, and for providing me with that all-important lucky break.

Damian, for his unique vision and creative talents, and for always being so willing to share both of them with me.

Mark, for being so generous, and for all those occasions when he has rescued me and my computer with his technical wizardry.

To my spiritual buddy Jon, for profound and thought-provoking conversations over steaming cappuccinos.

Debi, my fabulous best friend, for our overexcited coffee mornings, and for always being ready to skip with me through grassy fields in search of fairies and rainbows.

Julia McCutchen of Firefly Media, my fantastic publishing consultant.

And lastly to all my wonderful friends, whose support, love, encouragement, inspiration, and practical help has kept me sustained and motivated, and who bring pleasure and happiness to my life: Ali and Jase, Avril, Becka, Dave and Claire, Jan, Jeff, Julie, Karena, Kate, Gary, Mark, Neale, Paul and Emma, Shannon and Will, Steve and Lisa, Steve and Mickey, and Russell at the Quiet Mind Centre, Portsmouth.

To my editor Julie and everyone at Cyan Books, including Pom and Martin, who believed in this book and helped to make it a reality.

Introduction

"Who are you to write a spiritual book on heartbreak?"

That was the rather blunt and forthright question I was posed one night when a proud and enthusiastic friend introduced me as the "soon to be published author" of this very book.

Obviously it wasn't appropriate to bore the poor man with a blow-by-blow account of my life, so I just said, "Actually I have a great deal of experience on both counts." You might imagine that this was the start of a stimulating conversation on affairs of the heart or a deep discussion on the spiritual nature of life, but it wasn't. Eyebrows raised, head nodding vigorously, he replied, "That's good then" and changed the subject.

There are occasions when you are put on the spot and the right words fall from your mouth. With the benefit of time and hindsight I would not change the answer that I gave that night. I would say it again to you at this very minute. In this mixed-up crazy existence that we call life I think it's fair to say that I can wear the badge, cap, and T-shirt of "heartbreak survivor", as well as the "still learning" banner of the dedicated spiritual traveler.

What I am trying to say is that this book is written from experience. I know the pain of heartbreak, having nursed my own broken heart more times than I would actually care to admit. I know what it's like to feel sick with grief and to go through the motions of each day in a hollow, leaden blur of misery. I know what it's like to lie in bed unable to sleep as time slowly ticks by and the darkness of night creeps into the first rays of dawn. I know what it feels like to sit amid the shattered pieces of a broken life, overwhelmed, and daunted by what lies ahead.

Heartbreak is a hideous experience to go through no matter who you are or what age you are. Whether you are experiencing the pain of your first broken heart or the pain of separating after a lifetime together you have a choice to make. You can choose to take a passive role in your healing and hope that eventually the passage of time heals your wounds and mends your heart, or you can choose to be proactive in your healing and take a hand in your recovery.

As a lovelorn teenager I had no idea that I could be proactive in my healing process or of how I could help myself. Apart from always having had a reasonably sunny disposition and positive outlook I just let time run its course and muddled through as best I could. Several broken hearts and 20 years later my experience of heartbreak was entirely different. This time round, 15 years of spiritual work had given me an anchor deep within my soul to help me ride out the troubled waters of chaos. I had at my disposal a wealth of knowledge, resources, and tools to help me deal with my heartache. Armed with my spiritual toolbox I knew how to ease my pain, speed up my healing process, and keep my feet firmly on track to the light at the end of the tunnel.

Many months later, after I had emerged into that light at the end of the tunnel, a friend asked me whether I had any advice for her brokenhearted niece. Feeling very passionate about the whole subject, and knowing just what a significant difference even the smallest amount of spiritual work can do to ease a broken heart and aid recovery, I sent the young woman an email. The tips and ideas I suggested were the beginnings of this book.

As I planned this book I decided that there were six areas in which a spiritual perspective could have a dramatic impact on mending a broken heart. These became the six spiritual steps set out in this book. Each step reveals universal concepts that will inspire, enlighten, guide, and help you. They will empower you with knowledge and understanding, cast new light on your situation, and enable you to emerge from your heartbreak a wiser, richer, and stronger person. Instead of waiting for time to heal your wounds you will be able to take control of your recovery and add powerful spiritual elements to your healing process.

In order to get the most out of these six steps it might be useful for you to know a little more about two spiritual concepts that are integral to my outlook and upon which this book is based.

First, I believe that we are living in a world that focuses on the physical aspect of being. Bombarded by the media in a consumer-driven frenzy, we are in the midst of a spiritually arid time when it is easy for people to live in ignorance of their spirit. Yet it is my belief that we are far more than just a body that can think and feel, we are body, mind, *and spirit*.

I think that blended into the fabric of your physical, emotional, and mental body is a spiritual body, and at the heart of this is your spirit. Your spirit is the center of being, your divine heart, your heavenly connection to the universe and the world in which you live. Through your spirit you can open the doors to love, courage, peace, power, insight, and healing on a deeper and more profound level than you ever thought possible. In times of need, especially when you have a broken heart, your spirit is the greatest resource you have.

You don't need to have any prerequisites to unwrap, discover, or develop the magic of your spirit. You don't need to have a particular faith or to be a certain type of person to get the most out of the six steps. Being open to the possibility of new ideas and willing to look beyond your current understanding of life is the perfect start.

The second spiritual concept that is integral to this book can be summed up in one word: energy. Science lessons at school taught us that everything from chairs and tables to human bodies is made up of atoms of energy. While such a notion baffled me as a teenager, having now spent many years meditating and working spiritually my understanding of energy has profoundly changed.

I now realize that humans are incredibly complex and amazing beings comprised of energy. Your physical, mental, emotional, and spiritual bodies are made up of energy, and interlink through energy. While your physical body is made up of the densest energy, your spiritual body is made up of the most subtle and refined form of energy. This is why most people can see one and not the other! But it doesn't stop there; even your thoughts and emotions create their own unique vibrations of energy that ripple through your entire being.

Your physical, mental, emotional, and spiritual bodies are so subtly interlinked that it is impossible for a traumatic event like heartbreak not to touch each and every part. It was therefore really important to me to include within each of the six spiritual steps a range of tips, exercises, and suggestions that would enable you to nurture, nourish, and heal your mind, body, and spirit.

As I wrote the book these tips and ideas evolved into four distinct categories that I labeled Instant Soother, Body Balm, Practical DIY, and Picture This.

Instant Soother

The aim of Instant Soother is to offer you a diverse range of tools and techniques that can bring you instant solace and comfort. From power words, affirmations, crystals, essential oils, and boji stones to color therapy, music, and mind-training technology, there are lots of great tips and ideas that you will find incredibly effective, easy to use, and free if not reasonably priced. They are the perfect tonic to soothing the pain of heartbreak.

Body Balm

Body Balm offers you ideas on how you can help your physical body as it tries to cope with the impact of your stress and grief. During times of great mental and emotional distress it is very easy to neglect your body, and yet you depend on it every second of every day. Body Balm suggests ways in which you can support your body so that it, in turn, can support you through your time of need. From techniques on how to relax, release anger, and deal with insomnia to fitness, vitamins, nutrition, herbal and flower remedies, the ideas on offer are low cost, simple to do, and extremely beneficial. You will be able to nurture and nourish your body so that it stays healthy, and also plays an active role in supporting and enhancing its own healing process.

Practical DIY

Practical DIY is your chance to get active and start doing! There are lots of hands-on tasks that offer ideas on transforming your home and your life. Through exercises you will be able to explore issues such as change, self-love, mindfulness, patterns, partners, relationships, detachment, dreams, and goal setting. These tasks will enable you to cast new light on yourself and your life experiences. Your self-awareness and understanding will blossom and, as a result, you will be in the best possible position to make successful decisions for the future. Such insight is priceless but the process might not always be comfortable. While some of these exercises will be straightforward and quick, others might require a little more thought, time, and effort, and some could be quite a challenge. All of them, however, are totally worth doing for they will bring you the gifts of discovery, enlightenment, and healing.

Picture This

Picture This invites you to tap into the healing potential of your imagination. It is often said that where thought goes, energy flows. What this means is that whatever you imagine you can actually manifest and bring into being. For this reason creative visualizations are an incredibly powerful tool that you can use to heal your body, mind, and spirit. In this book, a host of different creative visualizations are on offer; you can pick from topics such as grief, healing, letting go, staying positive, to peace, balance, success, and spiritual connection. The wonderful thing about creative visualizations is that not only are they amazingly effective, they are also free to do and highly flexible: you can do them anywhere, anytime! By trying the creative visualizations on offer you will be able to harness the power of your mind and actively work on mending your broken heart. You will be able to enhance your body's natural healing process, nurture your spirit, and move forward to new and exciting possibilities.

Enjoy dipping in and trying out the ideas on offer in Instant Soother, Body Balm, Practical DIY, and Picture This. Feel free to mix and match the different tips and suggestions from the different steps; there is something for every aspect of your being and, just as importantly, something for every mood, state, or phase you may find yourself in. By trying them all you will be able to select the ones that are particularly successful for you and, in doing so, create your own unique spiritual toolbox. There is a Handy Hints section at the back of the book to give you further ideas on how to use crystals, essential oils, creative visualizations, and flower remedies.

There is no set way to use this book. You can start with Step 1 and work through to Step 6; alternatively, you can go straight to the step that you feel you need the most. Don't worry if you come across an idea or concept that you cannot accept or agree with. Embrace the concepts and ideas that feel right and let the ones that don't slip away. If you come across something that you are not yet ready to face, give yourself time: you can always come back to it at a later point.

Remember that there are no hard-and-fast rules in the process of grieving or recovery. You must do what you think feels right and allow yourself to be guided by your intuition. Do not try to rush your healing: be flexible and kind with yourself, give yourself permission to have good days and bad, and do not set unrealistic expectations for yourself in terms of how much, what, and by when you should achieve things.

By picking up this book you have already demonstrated an active commitment to do all you can to help yourself. You have taken a significant step forward. Now let me show you how to continue with your good intentions and mend the pieces of your broken heart. Let me share with you the knowledge, tools, and techniques that can heal your wounds and transform your life.

Whether you realize it or not you are at the beginning of an empowering and enlightening journey of survival and recovery. One day you will measure this journey not in the steps you have taken but in the miles you have traveled. You will be able to look back with a heart that is strong, whole, and abundant, and a body, mind, and spirit that has been restored to health and vitality. You will be proud of how much you have learnt, what you have achieved, and the progress you have made.

Starting your journey of recovery is astoundingly simple, for as the famous Buddhist saying explains, it begins with a single step. I invite you now to start with Six Spiritual Steps and begin your healing process.

Step 1

— ■ —

Calm your Soul: Soothe your Aching Heart

Suffering with a broken heart is one of the most painful experiences you can go through, and right now you are probably feeling overwhelmed and consumed with despair, hurt, loss, and misery. If it feels as if your world has ended and that you are going out of your mind with grief here are some facts that you need to know right away:

- ♥ nothing is insurmountable—even heartbreak
- ♥ what you are feeling is perfectly normal
- ♥ you are coping and you will continue to cope
- ♥ you have all the resources you need to get through it
- ♥ the pain will ease, life will settle down, and you will laugh again.

It might feel like your life has ended but in fact you have just reached the end of another chapter in your life's story. Overwhelmed with grief it is very hard to see yourself in the future well, whole, and happy, and it's hard to imagine you will ever recover. But grief is not everlasting: it is a process that you will move through, it is a journey of letting go, healing, moving forward, and recovery. You will adapt, you will heal, you will get over your ex, and the sun will shine again in your world.

The first thing that you need to do is to start believing that you will make a full and complete recovery. You are a product of all that you think, so start creating your future success right away with the power of positive thinking. Even if you struggle to believe that this is true you can still empower your healing process by being open to the possibility of making a full recovery.

Another thing to remember is that everything you are feeling and experiencing is perfectly *normal*. Don't be frightened by the maelstrom of emotions, thoughts, and feelings that are bombarding you. Do not be unnerved if everything feels surreal, your entire world

Instant Soother

Power words

Power words are those that can immediately transform dark and depressing thoughts and emotions. If you are consumed with thoughts about hate, your power word would be love; for anger you could use peace; for upset you could use calm. Hold the word at the forefront of your mind, allowing all other emotions and thoughts to disappear. If it helps you can visualize the word in large, colored letters, alternatively you can say or sing the word, you can even focus on the feelings and sensations the word produces. You might not notice a dramatic change by doing this instant soother but where the mind goes energy flows, whether you can feel it or not you have just succeeded in filling every fiber of your being with the energy of your power word.

Other power words you might like to use include acceptance, balance, courage, energy, faith, forgiveness, harmony, hope, insight, purification, truth, understanding, and wisdom.

Some Simple Dos and Don'ts of Heartbreak

Do:

♥ be gentle and kind to yourself, have the courage to admit you're vulnerable

♥ go with the flow of your emotions

♥ rest, nap, and sleep as much as you need

♥ listen to what your body and your instincts are telling you

♥ talk to compassionate and trustworthy friends, family members, and colleagues

♥ accept help, support, comfort, and love from those willing to offer them.

Try not to:

♥ belittle, ignore, or deny how you feel, give in gracefully to your emotions

♥ act as if nothing has happened—let those around know what you're going through

♥ fight the inevitable and waste your energy; face the truth of the situation

♥ add to the chaos of the moment by making additional changes

♥ make any decisions that you don't actually need to

is turned upside down, or if you feel totally over-whelmed. You are suffering with a broken heart and for a while at least life is bound to be traumatic.

Body Balm

Vitamins A, B, C, and E, as well as the minerals zinc and selenium help to support the body when it is under stress. Some of the foods that contain these important vitamins and minerals include sesame and pumpkin seeds, kiwi fruit and plums, as well as tomatoes, green vegetables, and seafood.

Heartache is more than just a word used to describe a state of mind, for some it is an actual physical pain in the chest—your heart really can ache. It is quite common to carry this aching, leaden heart around with you from the moment you wake to the moment you fall asleep. It is quite normal for your grief to overshadow every moment of your day, and for an all-consuming sadness to cloud your vision. Heartache leaves every-one feeling lost, bereft, and alone: it is a tangible, palpable sense of grief that cripples the sufferer physically, emotionally, and mentally. Heartache really is a heartbreaking business and if it does all get too much for you do not be afraid to go and get some professional help. There are many different avenues of help and support available to you, in the form of therapists, healers, practitioners, and counselors. You can look them up on the Internet or in your local telephone book.

The first reaction to the end of a relationship (even if you saw it coming) is shock. Shock can leave you feeling disoriented, dazed, and disconnected, and, if that is not enough to cope with, it often goes hand in hand

Practical DIY

Getting it down on paper

Writing about how you feel is a great form of personal expression and a very cathartic way of releasing your emotions. You can start writing a journal or a diary that tracks your road to recovery. It will help you to sort out your thoughts and feelings, and you will be able to look back and see the progress you have made.

with panic and fear. Do not be frightened if you swing between feeling bewildered and horrified, it is your body's way of taking on board the enormity of what is confronting you. The best thing that you can do for yourself when you feel gripped by anxiety is to try and calm yourself down, and the simplest way of doing this is to try the breathing exercise in the Body Balm box below. With a little practice you can learn to use your

Body Balm

Breathing exercises have an instant calming effect on the mind, body, and spirit. Amazingly simple and profoundly effective, you can do breathing exercises anywhere, anytime and no one need know what you're up to. Whenever you need to calm down and relax simply inhale for a count of five (six or seven if comfortable), hold for a count of five (six or seven) and then exhale for a count of five (six or seven). If you wish to develop the exercise, begin to imagine that as you exhale all the tension in your body is being released and that on every inhalation you are drawing peace and calm into your body.

breath as a way to take control of your body, and soothe your fears and anxieties. Breathing is an incredibly effective life tool.

Disbelief, denial, confusion, and numbness are also common reactions to the loss of a partner. "I can't believe it," "It can't be true," "I don't know what's happening," "I feel empty" are common thoughts to have. Do not worry if this is how you feel, it is your mind reeling at the news, and is a natural response to the mental and emotional trauma you are facing. Do not add to your discomfort by fighting, questioning, or analyzing how you feel; go with the flow and as far as possible just let yourself be.

As reality sinks in, shock, disbelief, and numbness move on to a diverse multitude of other thoughts, feelings, and emotions. This is when the grieving process really starts and when the pain really sets in. People grieve in different ways: for some it is intense feelings of despair, loss, fear, pain, and loneliness; for others it is helplessness, disillusionment, misery, emptiness, disbelief, and even anger. It is quite natural to flit from one emotion to another, and to go through a hundred different emotions in an hour and a thousand different

Practical DIY

Lightening the load

When suffering with a broken heart trying to cope with life's normal routines and aggravations can be a huge challenge. At this difficult time make yourself top priority and do all you can to lighten your load. Here are some ideas to get you started.

1. *Prioritize those things that **must** be done, those things that **should** be done, those things that **could** be done, and those things that can definitely wait.*

2. *What can you cut, trade, chop, change, delegate, relegate, alter, buy in, hire, reduce, or ignore to make life a little easier for you?*

3. *Say "yes" to those people who care about you and want to offer you a helping hand.*

4. *Say "no" to new projects, duties, tasks, or responsibilities.*

5. *Plan your time and arrange visits to friends, and activities that will keep you occupied. Get active and get moving—go for a walk, a swim, or to the movies. You can even spoil yourself with a luxury like a massage or a manicure.*

emotions in a day. What you must remember is that grief enables you to mourn the loss of your partner, the loss of your relationship, and the loss of all the hopes, dreams, and expectations you had. Only by going through the grieving process will you be able to sever the ties of attachment to your ex-partner, heal your pain, set yourself free, and move on with your life.

The most important thing that you can do is to admit that you are hurt, and to acknowledge and express your feelings and emotions. It is OK to feel depressed. It is OK to feel frightened. It is OK to feel angry and it is OK to feel guilty. Never forget that your emotions are a natural part of the healing process and need the freedom to flow and to move. Allow yourself to "just be" and do not restrict yourself with expectations and barriers. Every emotion that passes through you is telling you something. Only if you listen to what your body is telling you will you be connected with all that is going on inside of you. You can learn a great deal from your pain and discomfort.

No matter how much pain you are in, be brave and stick with it. Do not try to bury yourself with distractions, do not avoid, dodge, repress, pretend, or cover

Picture This

Help to heal your heart

The following creative visualization offers an amazing way to connect with your heart and take a proactive role in its healing process. Sit down and close your eyes. Relax by following the gentle flow of your breath. When you are ready, begin to visualize your hands gently cupped together resting in your lap. Next reach up with your hands and tenderly scoop up your heart. Hold your heart in your hands, allowing your love and your wishes of healing to flow to it in the form of blue, pink, or even multi-colored rays of light. Imagine the rays of light flowing in and through your heart, nurturing and healing it. When you are finished, gently return your heart to your chest.

up your emotions. If you refuse to acknowledge your pain you are wallpapering over the reality of your situation and you will ultimately prolong your suffering.

If you do deny, minimize, or ignore your pain it does not miraculously vanish. Emotion that is not allowed

Body Balm

Bach Flower Remedies offer the following essences.

♥ *If you are feeling despair and hopelessness try Gorse.*
♥ *If you are experiencing shock and grief try Star of Bethlehem.*
♥ *If you feel you are at the limits of endurance and suffering with deep despair try Sweet Chestnut.*

expression sits and waits until the day comes when it can no longer be ignored any more and it explodes. Suppressed pain and emotion can trigger mental and psychological breakdown, as well as a host of other bodily ailments. The best time to deal with pain is when it happens, not weeks, months, or even years later. Do yourself a favor—acknowledge and accept your pain and sadness *now*.

Remember that to grieve, to cry, and mourn are the normal responses to the loss of a loved one. You are not weak, pathetic, or foolish for hurting. Your pain is there for a reason: it is there because you loved someone very deeply and invested a great deal of your love, time, energy, and faith in them. You have every right to experience an enormous sense of loss when they withdraw from your life. Even if you have been the one to choose to end the relationship you still have the right to grieve and mourn.

Body Balm

Anger is a natural response to pain, but not a very healthy emotion to carry around for any length of time. The best thing to do with anger is to vent it—get it out of your system. If you are at home, pummel and beat a pile of cushions or pillows, or do some very strenuous exercise such as kickboxing, jogging, or playing squash. Jumping up and down on a box of cereal can be immensely satisfying, albeit messy.

In fact you might be interested to know that the depth to which you are capable of experiencing genuine sorrow and heartbreak is also the depth to which you can experience joy and love. Sorrow and joy are the mirrored reflections of the peaks and troughs of our emotional capacity. The extent to which you are currently grieving is in fact a measure of the depth of love, commitment, and energy that you are capable of experiencing.

Another thing that can happen when pain tugs at your heart is for previous hurts to come to the fore. Past experiences of loss can resurface and you find yourself mourning other periods of pain as well as the current situation you are in. This is normal and if it allows buried or previously unresolved hurt to be released and cleansed from your body then, in the long term, it can only be a positive thing.

At this difficult time it is best to lower your expectations about what you can achieve as you are likely to be distracted, to make mistakes, to be less productive, to overreact, and to be extremely fragile. Do not be surprised if the aggravations and irritations of life that you usually take in your stride are too much to cope with and knock you off balance. Your tolerance threshold is likely to be reduced and it is probable that you won't feel, seem, appear, or be like your normal self. Small things can push you over the edge and be "the straw that breaks the camel's back". You are quite likely to be short-tempered, grumpy, snappy,

Instant Soother

Essential oils can be used to great effect on your body, mind and spirit.

- ♥ *To promote inner peace try chamomile.*
- ♥ *To calm a troubled mind and turbulent emotions try marjoram.*
- ♥ *To quieten down your mind try sandalwood.*
- ♥ *Reduce shock and fear with neroli or peppermint.*

emotional, unstable, erratic, and moody, as well as a whole host of other unusual or exacerbated conditions. This is to be expected and if other people know what is going on in your life they will make allowances for you. Do the same for yourself and, within reason, "cut yourself some slack."

Tears are part of your body's natural healing process: they help to cleanse. Do not be ashamed of your tears and, wherever possible, do not inhibit them: cry if you feel like crying. The problem is, however, that grief does not respect where you are or what you're doing: emotion can cause tears to well up and catch you off

Picture This

Let go of your pain

The following creative visualization offers a wonderful way to release the pain of heartbreak and will help lighten your load.

Sit down and close your eyes. Relax by following the gentle flow of your breath. When you are ready, begin to visualize a table in front of you on which there is a magic pen, a piece of paper, a golden box, and a large helium balloon tied by a golden ribbon to a crystal weight.

In your mind begin saying how you feel, listing all the different words that express your heartache. As you talk so the magic pen writes down everything you say on the piece of paper. In this way everything you are feeling and thinking pours out of you and onto the paper. When you have finished put the piece of paper inside the golden box. Next untie the ribbon holding the helium balloon from the crystal weight and tie it around the golden box. Hold the golden box high in the air saying, "I release my pain and ask the universe to take my burdens and to shine its heavenly light onto my heart." Visualize the balloon carrying off your pain to the universe and the golden light of the universe shining down on you. Repeat this exercise as many times as you like.

guard at the most inappropriate moments. If you are in a situation where you cannot let go and cry then at least make sure that you acknowledge the feelings that have stirred by silently saying to the emotion or thought that has arisen "Yes, I feel you." In this way you are consciously telling your body that you are listening to it even if you can do nothing about it at that moment. If you can't cry because you are at work can you disappear for a short while and go for a breath of fresh air, or can you grab a pen and paper and write down what's going through your mind?

If you feel like you need a few days off work and you can take the time off without creating more problems for yourself, then do so. Do not allow this to slip into weeks though. No matter how hard it is to go through the normal schedule of work when your life is in a million pieces it does enforce order and routine within your daily life. It also offers an escape from being totally consumed by your misery. However, throwing yourself into work all hours of the day and night in an attempt to avoid the pain you are feeling can also be detrimental. Any attempt to divert the pain only prolongs the agony.

Practical DIY

Getting it off your chest

Talking is a therapeutic way of coping with heartbreak. If you have lots of people to talk to that's great, but if you don't find talking easy or you don't have anyone you feel you can talk to, you might like to buy a dictaphone or a cassette recorder and some blank tapes. Chat to the dictaphone, verbalizing your thoughts and feelings. You can either keep the tapes to record your journey or re-record over them as you go.

The reality for millions of us is that no matter how grief stricken and wretched we feel, the endless treadmill of life rumbles on and we have no choice but to keep going. When you find yourself brokenhearted but unable to take time out from the demands of life it is vital that you set aside some real, private time for yourself. It need only be 5 to 10 minutes a day but you must create a space where you are not someone's boss, colleague, relative, friend, or parent. You need to make time where there is no pretence, no show, no effort, a time where you can touch base with the real you and what you are feeling. The quieter you are, the more you can hear.

When your heart is aching it is easy to think of nothing else and to get consumed by your pain. Try to remember that you and your life are more than just this particular period of suffering. Try to step back and visualize this moment as one piece of a much larger jigsaw puzzle of the life that you have had and still want to have.

In a world where time "is money" and "of the essence" we are not in the habit of waiting very long for any-

Body Balm

Suffering with insomnia? Try eating fish with green vegetables for your evening meal. Both foods are rich in calcium and magnesium so they help to balance your brain's chemistry and relax your body. Have a bath just before bedtime and mix a few drops of lavender or thyme essential oil in the water. A mug of hot milk also works.

Practical DIY

A little bit of "you time"

It is important for you to make time in your busy life to have some peace and quiet, some time alone with yourself when you can touch base with your true self. Here are a few ideas to get you started.

1. *Cycling, swimming, and walking all offer healthy, active moments where you could focus your awareness on yourself. By emptying your mind and focusing deeply on each movement that you take, you could turn your keep-fit time into a time of reflection and inner connection.*

2. *Set aside 15 minutes in the morning, at lunchtime, or in the evening to be alone and quiet. Sit in a comfy chair and listen to classical music or specially created tranquility/meditative music. Keep your awareness on the music and let unwanted thoughts fall away.*

thing. Nearly everything we want is at our fingertips: we don't even have to get out of our cars to pick up our fast food. With everything we need at our disposal we can have very false expectations of how much time it takes to mend a broken heart. What we want is to fix it like we can fix everything else: we want a speedy and smooth road to recovery. The heart cannot be fixed in this way, it needs to heal itself in its own unique fashion. It is far better not to set up unrealistic expectations for yourself but rather to go with the flow.

Instant Soother

Try affirmations to help you work through your feelings.

♥ *I grant permission for myself to grieve and in doing so I enable healing to take place.*
♥ *My heart is healing and I am getting stronger.*
♥ *I am open to the possibility of healing and a new beginning.*

Most of us find the road to mending a broken heart a challenging one. There will be peaks and troughs, good days and bad, setbacks and advancements, smooth periods and tough times. This is the nature of healing and unfortunately there are no shortcuts, all you can do is keep on keeping on, and slowly and steadily you will cover the necessary ground and make emotional progress.

Do not be disconcerted when an unexpected comment, a significant date, a memory or a wave of unexpected emotion rises up, takes hold and knocks you backwards. Accept these times with resignation and see them not as setbacks but as another layer of your grief rising to the surface to be released.

Do not expect any sudden and dramatic changes—healing is a gradual process. However, with patience and commitment you will heal and as you do so a new whole, stronger, and wiser you will emerge.

All you can do when pain is wrenching at your heart is to work with it by trying the tips and exercises presented in this chapter; repeat them as often as possible and, if you can, incorporate them into your daily routine. If you can do this then gradually, as the days and weeks pass, you will find that the intensity of your pain abates. The moments in between your anguish and your pain will grow and gradually peace will replace chaos, wholeness will replace emptiness, and the dark clouds of despair will disappear in sunshine.

$Step$ 2

— ∎ —

Stay Ahead of the Game: What Goes Around Comes Around

Suffering with a broken heart can seem like a never-ending path of emotional pain and mental chaos. You can end up wondering whether you are ever going to feel normal again or if life will ever get better. One very simple truth that might put a new slant on your heartbreak is that your recovery actually lies in your own hands. The thoughts, feelings, emotions, intentions, goals, and aspirations that you create go a long way to shape your reality and mold not only your day-to-day experiences but also how your future will unfold. It is up to you whether you mend your broken heart or allow it to remain broken.

Many people view heartbreak as something that has happened to them at the hands of another person. What is overlooked in the comment "he/she broke my heart" is personal responsibility. Your heart belongs to you. The fact that it is broken is not the fault of another person, it is the consequence of a decision that you made to take a lover. Just as it was your decision to get into this now broken relationship it is up to you to decide

Instant Soother

Every crystal is unique in the energetic properties it has to offer. Try the following.

♥ *For cleansing and absorbing negative energy try using amethyst.*
♥ *For grounding and energizing of the physical body try using hematite.*
♥ *For release of emotional and physical tension try moonstone.*
♥ *To help boost the immune system and release toxins and stress try using turquoise.*

how you react to what has happened. What is more important than who broke whose heart, is what *you* are going to do about it.

Life is all about making choices. Every second of every day, every week, every month, every year, we make thousands upon thousands of choices. Mixed in with the many mundane, trivial, and routine choices are major life choices. Right now at this very moment you are facing possibly one of the biggest life choices you will ever have to make. What are you going to do with your broken heart? Far from being a passive experience healing is very much an active process: if you do nothing, nothing will happen; if you set your mind to action you will manifest change. You can choose to become ensnared in anger, bitterness, jealousy, hate, and even revenge, or you can choose to focus your energy on mending your broken heart and making a full, glorious, and inspirational recovery.

The most powerful tool you have at your disposal to mend your broken heart is positive thinking. As doctors around the world can testify, a "fighting spirit" combined with a resilient determination to get better are the crucial factors in patients making a full recovery.

Picture This

Stay positive

The following creative visualizations are quick and effective to do, each focuses on bringing some positive energy into your being through the symbol of light.

1. *Visualize your problem or your pain as a dark, solid mass. Visualize the golden rays of the universe shining down on you, transforming the dark mass into a golden, radiant light.*
2. *Visualize a huge glowing golden sun above you; picture its warm, healing and energizing rays shining down upon you. Imagine the golden rays pouring into your mind and your heart, and see your dark thoughts and pain disappearing in the beautiful light.*

You might not have visible wounds but you have suffered major heart trauma and you too need to adopt a tenacious resolve to recover. The more positive you can be about your recovery the more you will empower the healing process taking place within you.

Being positive is such a powerful healing force because of the incredible connection that exists between the mind and the body. Your physical, emotional, mental, and spiritual bodies are as closely interwoven as the fibers of the clothes you are wearing. If you are in any doubt about the connection that exists between the mind and the body then consider the following experiences. What about blushing when you are embarrassed, getting butterflies in your stomach when you are nervous, or your heart lurching if you spot your ex's car? Each one of these reactions proves to you the unbelievably rapid connection that exists between thoughts, emotions, feelings, and the body.

The intimate relationship that exists between the mind and the body is founded on energy. Every thought, feeling, and emotion you have creates its own unique vibration of energy. This energy travels instantly through your entire physical and spiritual body, touching every cell and fiber of your being. If you think positive thoughts you flood your body with the vibrational energy of positivity; if, however, you think negative thoughts you flood your body with the vibrational energy of negativity.

Body Balm

Grieving is a tiring process that requires a great deal of physical, mental, and emotional energy. As well as getting a good night's sleep, eating well will help you to cope better with the stress and angst of heartbreak. Try to go for healthy foods such as fruit, vegetables, whole-grain cereals and breads, lean white meat, fish, and fiber. If you can't eat try making pure fruit smoothies, or buy some supplement shakes. They are easy to drink and are enriched with protein, vitamins and minerals.

Everything you experience emotionally and mentally affects the health of your body, and many of the ailments that afflict us are the physical expression of "dis-ease" within the mind. Often the health of your body is a reflection of the health of your mind, and this is why it is so important for you to be positive.

If the sight of your ex's car causes your heart to lurch and your stomach to do a somersault, then what effect do you think dark, negative, and possibly even malevolent thoughts and emotions have on your body? Do you really want the negative energies of anger, hatred, and jealousy flowing through every fiber and cell of your body? No, of course you don't, and this is why you must not allow yourself to dwell in a negative space any more than is absolutely necessary.

Journeying through the pain of a broken heart you will of course experience many mixed emotions and there will be times when you will feel very low. This is a natural part of the healing process and should be accepted as such. It is important to be sympathetic and kind to yourself but you must be vigilant and not

Instant Soother

Where your thought goes energy flows. This means that as soon as you think something you immediately make an energetic connection to it. Try to raise your thoughts up to heaven. Ask heaven, the angels, or Jesus to:

♥ *give you strength and courage*
♥ *ease your pain*
♥ *give you the help that you need.*

allow yourself to overindulge in negativity or become trapped in a victim mentality. You are not being asked to become a paragon of virtue but to stay alert to the phases, moods, thoughts, and feelings that you harbor.

Picture This

Set negative thoughts and feelings free

The following creative visualization is highly effective at getting rid of unwanted thoughts and emotions.

Step 1

As soon as you realize that you are thinking or feeling something negative say clearly (out loud or in your head), "I release this negative thought/feeling."

Step 2

Visualize the thought or feeling sprouting wings and flying out of your mind, or body. Watch it flying higher and higher into the sky and disappearing. Fill the void left behind with golden light.

Repeat this exercise as often as you need.

Do not allow the seeds of bitterness, hate, anger, and other such negative states of being to bury their roots in your damaged heart. Always remember that what you direct your thoughts to grows.

Transient phases of negativity are a natural part of the healing process; they will not do you any long-term damage. However, dark, destructive, and negative thoughts that are nurtured, repressed, ignored, or buried restrict your healing, impede your recovery, harden your heart, and ultimately can make you ill. Unvented negative emotion does not disappear: it turns inward, becomes embodied, and eventually manifests itself as illness.

By being positive you not only enhance your body's natural healing process, you also send out a clear statement of optimistic intent to your subconscious mind. Your conscious mind is the logical, reasoning, rational part of your brain—whatever you are "consciously" aware of at any given moment. Your subconscious mind is *everything else*. It is easy to view the conscious and subconscious as two separate elements, however they are far more interconnected than that and the easiest way to understand them is to picture an iceberg. Your

Practical DIY

Positive reminders

It is important to keep positive and remain focused on your healing and recovery. Here are some ideas on how you can keep that positive focus going.

1. *Make a list of all the positive, successful things that you can do, have achieved, or enjoyed in your life—everything from educational, personal, professional to amazing moments, experiences, and people. Nothing is too big or too small to include. Pin your list somewhere safe and, if needs be, private to remind yourself of all the good times that you have had.*
2. *Write a list of five things that are positive in your life right at this very moment—it might include your friends, family, children, pet, home, or work. Don't lose sight of what you have that is great.*
3. *Find a photo or an image of a good memory, an uplifting moment, a great achievement, or a wonderful time in your life. Stick it where you can see it regularly and enjoy an emotional boost.*

conscious mind is the tip of the iceberg poking out above the sea water. Your subconscious mind is the massive underwater structure that makes up the body of the iceberg. Where one ends and the other begins cannot truly be defined for they belong to the whole that makes up who you are.

Your subconscious mind is everything that you are apart from what you are consciously focusing on. It is the main body of your thoughts, attitudes, philosophy, and belief systems. It is also responsible for all your autonomic body functions, such as breathing and digestion. It is the center that takes over when you switch off and go into autopilot. It is your subconscious mind that drives your car while you drift off.

Body Balm

Get active. Go to the gym, walk, swim, join an exercise or dance class. Not only will exercise enhance your fitness, promote good sleep, and increase your energy, it also releases endorphins (your body's happiness chemicals), which are known to dispel negative mental states.

Your subconscious mind is creative, imaginative, and full of marvelous resources that can help you, but like a small child it needs direction and guidance. Unaware of this, as most of us are, we all unwittingly lead it in the wrong direction. Instead of channeling its resources and using the power of the subconscious to improve our life, we program it with limiting beliefs as well as fears, anxieties, and worries. These in turn feed back into the conscious mind and a cyclical pattern of negativity is created. The best time to program your subconscious mind with affirmations and creative visualizations is when it is in the alpha state. To help you reach the alpha state of serenity and calm, practice the relaxation breathing exercise in Step 1 (see page 7).

The good news is that you can reprogram your subconscious mind simply by leading it in the right direction with empowering, healing, and positive suggestions in the form of simple words, affirmations, pictures, and images. Invite your subconscious to join you in your journey and in your recovery.

Take a good look at the thoughts, feelings, emotions, ideas, and belief systems that you have; look at the patterns running through your life. Pay particular

Picture This

Creating future history

This creative visualization offers you the opportunity to project yourself forward into the future and see yourself fully recovered, flourishing, and fulfilled.

Sit down and close your eyes. Relax by following the gentle flow of your breath. When you are ready to begin, visualize yourself at a party, entertaining friends, or celebrating the achievement of a long-term goal. Make the scene as real and detailed as you can. See how happy, healthy, and successful, content, confident, and fantastic you look and feel. Notice the twinkle in your eyes, the smile on your face, and the wonderful energy radiating out from you.

Repeat the exercise as often as possible, remembering that "what you think about, you create".

attention to those that keep recurring in your relationships, and reprogram anything that is unhelpful, negative, and unconstructive. Program your subconscious mind with the intention that you are making a full and inspirational recovery from your broken heart. Program it with the beautiful vision of the richer, wiser, and stronger person that is blossoming out of misfortune.

Another reason to be positive lies in the law of attraction and its basic premise that what you give out you attract back. If you remain consumed by negativity you will only ever draw negativity to you. The moment you reverse this and embrace positivity you empower the universe to move with you and, as a result, positive things will manifest for you. Like attracts like, it's as simple as that.

Instant Soother

They say that "what you give you get back." You can try this out for yourself with a smile. Even if you don't feel happy make the effort to smile at the people you work with and move among. You will be amazed at how many people return your smile and how such a simple action can lift your spirits.

Picture This

Set yourself free

Often it is our attachment to our ex-partner that causes us ongoing pain; when we let go of our ex we set ourselves free. Try the following creative visualization to sever the attachment and free yourself from the chains that bind. Sit down and close your eyes. Relax by following the gentle flow of your breath. When you are ready to begin, visualize a golden rope laid out in a figure of eight on the floor before you. Visualize yourself stepping into one end of the loop and, when you are ready, your ex stepping into the other end of the loop. Now ask the universe to provide you with a sword and see what materializes for you. Take the sword and gently cut through the rope, and as you do this say, "I set you free and in doing so I set myself free." Watch as your ex slowly drifts away from you. You might also like to thank the universe for its help and continued support.

As well as the law of attraction there is also the law of karma to consider. This is the law of cause and effect—whatever you do in thought, word, or deed will return to you. Phrases such as "what goes around comes around," "if you sow thorns, you cannot harvest corns," and "as ye sow so shall ye reap," each refer to this law. Everything that you think, feel, and do creates the fibers that weave the fabric of your future life.

The law of karma is exact: there is no getting away with anything. Karma teaches you the lesson of personal responsibility and it calls on you to strive for the highest level of goodness, compassion, love, and positivity that you can attain. Precise it might be but karma is not unfair: intent also needs to be considered. If you do something with the intention of hurting someone then you will create bad karma for yourself; if you unintentionally hurt someone then bad karma is not generated.

While some people might argue that you have every right to want revenge or that you are justified in feeling bitter, resentful, or angry, the truth is that such feelings are detrimental to you. As already explained, such negative feelings hinder your healing, impede your recovery, set down destructive programs in the subconscious, and cause you to attract negativity. Such

Picture This

Archangel Uriel

The Archangel Uriel is regarded as the most radiant of all the Archangels: he brings the gift of divine light to mankind. This fantastic creative visualization enables you to connect with Uriel to bring peace into your heart and find the light within.

Sit down and close your eyes. Relax by following the gentle flow of your breath. When you are ready, call upon the mighty Archangel Uriel for help—you might like to say, "Mighty Archangel Uriel please draw close to me and bring peace to my heart." Visualize Archangel Uriel in his purple, gold, and ruby robes drawing close behind you; imagine his wings wrapping around you so that these beautiful colors envelope you. Breathe in the beautiful colors and, as you do so, imagine that they flow down to your bruised heart. On your out breath imagine the pain, anger, or negativity flowing out of your heart and out of your body. Allow Uriel to take your pain away and fill your heart with peace, love, and light. When you are ready you will get a sense that Uriel is gently pulling his energy away from you. As he departs thank him for his love and help.

feelings also create bad karma and will only bring you unhappiness in the future.

No matter how much you have suffered as a result of your ex's behavior do not be fooled into believing that you are justified in seeking revenge, teaching them a lesson, or giving them what they deserve. It is not your responsibility to dole out punishment, and if you indulge in any "tit for tat" behavior you will only create bad karma for yourself. To ensure your own future happiness and well-being, try to rise above any such thoughts and deeds. Remember, you are not doing this for your ex, you are doing this for you.

The opposite of revenge is forgiveness and whilst this might seem a desperately hard idea to swallow it is where the heart of your healing and future well-being rests. Forgiveness is not about suffering fools gladly, being a doormat, condoning your ex's bad behaviour or coming round to the point of view that what they did was ok. Forgiveness is about letting go, releasing, and moving on. Believe it or not the first place you need to channel your forgiveness is with yourself.

At first glance you might think that you have done nothing that requires self-forgiveness but stop and

Picture This.

Working with your heart center

Try this lovely creative visualization to open up your heart center and tap in to the full potential of your love, forgiveness and compassion.

Sit down and close your eyes. Relax by following the gentle flow of your breath. When you are ready, visualize a beautiful green jewel (green is the color of the heart's energy center, but you can also use pink for unconditional love) buried within your heart. As the energy of your thoughts blends with the jewel, notice it begin to burn brightly and glow with iridescent light. Watch as the light given off by your jewel spills over and starts to illuminate your heart. The light is so bright and powerful that it spreads outward from your heart into your chest, and from there it washes outward over your entire body. Carry on until this light fills your whole body and encases you in an auric glow of green (or pink). When you are ready, imagine the light reducing and withdrawing back into your heart. Stop when you reach your jewel and leave it glowing, ready for the next time.

consider how you feel about what's happened. Look beneath the surface. If you feel cross, upset, disappointed, angry, frustrated, sad, ashamed, guilty or regretful about the relationship, the events, the experience or the choices that you have made then indeed you may well need to consider doing a little work on forgiving yourself.

Another way to look at this issue of forgiveness is to ask yourself some searching questions. Are you cross or disappointed with yourself for getting involved with your ex? Are you angry with yourself for falling for a looser, a timewaster, a philanderer, or someone who just wasn't deserving of your love? Are you annoyed with yourself for staying too long in the relationship or perhaps for quitting too early? Giving too much or not enough? For being deceived or being the deceiver? Often it is not immediately apparent that we need to work on self-forgiveness, however, it is a really crucial part of your healing process and of staying ahead of the game.

Only when you forgive yourself can you begin to forgive your ex, and you must do this to set yourself free at every level and in every sense of the word. The power of forgiveness acts as a miracle balm in healing your wounds and mending your broken heart. Even if right at this very moment it is something that you cannot entertain be at least open to the possibility that one day you might be able to extend forgiveness to your ex.

Affirmations, power words, creative visualizations, meditation, and the determination to embrace only that which is positive are the tools available to you. Do not forget that where thought goes, energy flows, so even now at this very minute you can begin working with your heart center just by thinking about it and directing your thoughts towards it. If you embrace positivity, compassion, and forgiveness, and fill your heart with love, not only will you totally recover from your broken heart, you will lay the karmic stepping stones for a future filled with love, fulfillment, and happiness. This might seem like a tall order but the key word here is "strive." Set your goals high and simply do the best you can.

The moment you decide you want to replace negativity with love, compassion, and forgiveness, the moment you choose to embrace a more spiritual outlook in the affairs of your heart, the divine flame in your soul begins to shine more brightly. The universe sees this light and draws closer to you. Understanding your pain, desires, intentions, and dreams the universe moves with you to help you achieve your goals, aspirations, and endeavors. You can further empower your actions by calling on the universe to help you. Ask for the universe's help in mending your broken heart, in keeping your thoughts, words, and deeds positive and in helping you to forgive yourself and your ex.

What you do with your broken heart is up to you: you can either make a full and inspirational recovery and set a shining example to others or you can remain static or even wallow in self-pity, misery, and despair. The most empowering tool that you have at your disposal is positivity. Using positivity you can nurture your broken heart back to full strength and create a future for yourself that is full of happiness, fulfilment, and potential. Positivity works on every level of your being—it makes a difference to you physically, mentally, emotionally, and spiritually. It affects your mind, body, and soul.

Your intention shapes your recovery and, ultimately, your future. All you need to do to begin to experience the wonders that positivity can bring to your heartbreak is to turn your back on negativity and walk in the opposite direction, toward the sun.

Step 3

— ∎ —

Accepting Change:
What Will Be Will Be

When we fall in love we begin a wonderful, exciting, and joyful ride sitting high on the crest of life's wave. The rosy spectacles of love tint our vision and it is easy to be happy, positive, and fearless. The filter of love enables us to see the world from a whole new perspective, all the struggles, irritations, doubts, and worries that existed before still exist, yet the love bursting from our hearts washes over everything with well-being. Although we might speak about our good fortune we rarely stop to analyze, assess, and chew over what has happened to us. Instead we get swept up in the moment, go with the flow, and instinctively try to get the most out of every second.

Body Balm

Try some ancient herbal remedies to soothe your nerves and calm your fears.

St John's wort: *calms, soothes, and restores the nervous system. Ideal for periods of stress, anxiety, nervous depletion, fatigue, and exhaustion.*

Passion flower: *eases muscular tension brought on through anxiety, as well as nervous insomnia.*

Hyssop, lemon balm, wild lettuce, and rosemary: *alleviate anxiety and tension. Rosemary also helps relieve tension headaches.*

The minute that life takes a turn for the worse however, we find ourselves using a very different frame of reference. In the battleground of separation, instead of applying the same principles as before we tend to change tack. We don't accept what has happened to us, we don't skim the surface and go with the flow; instead we wrestle with the challenges confronting us and resist the changes taking place. As well as becoming negative, we also analyze, dissect, resist, and fight

Practical DIY

Crystal bathing

Simply place your crystal directly in the bath, then lie back and relax so that you can enjoy the unique healing energy it has to offer. Lots of smaller crystals can go in a bag. Try using:

- ♥ *rose quartz for peace and calm, and to soothe your broken heart*
- ♥ *citrine for balancing and aligning, personal power, and energizing*
- ♥ *cornelian to help overcome feelings of sadness and fear, and to boost physical and inner strength*
- ♥ *smoky quartz to lift your spirits.*

what has taken place. We don't flow with the unfolding events; instead, we stop dead in our tracks.

The most important thing you can do when faced with a broken heart and a relationship that has ended is to accept what has happened. Fighting the situation will not help you in any way. It will block your energy, impede your recovery, manifest negativity in mind, body, and spirit, and add to the burden you are already facing. Putting up any form of resistance and fighting the inevitable will only make your pain greater and put you under even more physical, emotional, mental, and spiritual stress and strain. At such a difficult time it is your duty to do all you can to help yourself and follow the path of least resistance.

This path challenges you to be brave and strong, to have the courage to face the truth, and flow with the sad and painful events taking place in your life. Place your trust in the infinite wisdom of the universe and accept that you are in the right place, at the right time and that, even if you cannot see it for yourself, your life is unfolding as it should. Draw strength from the knowledge that everything happens for a reason, and what will be will be.

Like a pond that stagnates if its water cannot move, your energy needs to flow and move freely. By having the courage to accept the situation you are in and allowing yourself to go with the flow of life, not only do you ensure that you are moving in harmony with the universe but also your energy is free to move where it needs to go. If you fight and resist the situation you block your energy and, just like the stagnant pond, you too will gradually clog up and become unhealthy. If you restrict your ability to experience pain you will also restrict your ability to enjoy happiness and pleasure.

Instant Soother

Findhorn Flower Essences Sacred Space, and Crystal Clear by Petal Tone Essences have been specially designed to cleanse negative energy and harmonize the energies in your home.

So why is it that we tend to react so badly to breakups? One answer is fear. Fear is possibly the most negative, destructive, and damaging emotion we are capable of feeling, and there are many different things to feel afraid of when a relationship ends: you can be frightened of the depth of pain and sense of loss you are experiencing; you might be afraid of what is going to happen and whether you will be able to cope; you may be afraid of being alone, unloved, or unable to love; or you may fear that you might never recover from the breakup. Everything can be daunting and frightening, and seem totally overwhelming.

Picture This

Facing your fears

The positive affirmations in the following exercise can empower you to be whatever you need to be.

Lacking courage	— *I am brave.*
Fear of independence	— *I am strong, independent, and in control.*
Fear of the future	— *I trust the universe will provide for all my needs.*
Fearfulness	— *I am fearless. I can achieve anything I set my mind to.*
Feeling inadequate	— *I am complete.*

Say your affirmation/s then ask yourself "What is it like to be [the positive state you wish to achieve]?" For example, if you are working on courage, ask yourself "What is it like to be courageous?", and enjoy experiencing what that's like.

The problem is that fear cripples and paralyzes. It is totally destructive and will always do its best to inhibit you from facing challenges and prevent you growing. Fear also causes distress, anxiety, and stress at a time when you are already hurt, and your innate reaction to feel fearful merely adds to your existing pain. The ironic thing is that our fears are usually much worse than the actual reality.

The first thing you need to do is to stop reacting to your fear and instead stand still. In the silence and the quietness spend a little while listening to what your fear is saying to you. Adopt the attitude that your fear is teaching you something about yourself. What exactly are you afraid of? Is it rejection, change, loss, aloneness, or resentment, for example? The moment that you realize where your fear or fears lie is an empowering point in your life because now you can begin to end fear's reign of power over you. Use affirmations, creative visualizations, and power words to reprogram your fear and set yourself free. Become the master of your mind and take control.

The civilized world is driven by the great powers of the media. We are bombarded from every direction with

Instant Soother

InnerTalk has created a patented system of mind-training technology in which positive affirmations are hidden within the sound-tracks of nature or music CDs. There are over 200 titles available, including Forgiving and Letting Go *as well as* Accepting Change, Loss of a Loved One, *and* Healing the Past. *All you need to do is play the CDs as background music or even as you sleep. They are fantastic. Go to the website www.innertalk.co.uk for more information.*

expensive marketing campaigns aimed at brainwashing us into buying the products, ideals, and lifestyles on offer. The idea that we can control life and protect ourselves from anything untoward is continually repeated on gigantic billboards, in glossy magazines, and on TV and radio airwaves. We can insure practically any-thing—from our bodies, lives, houses, belongings, cars, and pets to burst pipes and credit cards. We can even safeguard our children by providing them with mobile/cell phones so they can "stay in touch." Even if anything untoward does happen we are used to help

being just a phone call (and debit card swipe) away—
we can buy in a solution to our problem and get it
fixed. Doesn't this make life seem so easy?

The truth is that although we can buy in to all these different insurance policies, although we can go out and

---

Picture This

Protection

*At this vulnerable time, use the power of creative
visualization to protect yourself.*

As you go about your daily life, visualize yourself:

- ♥ *fully enclosed in a gigantic bubble*
- ♥ *standing behind a full-length shield*
- ♥ *wearing a full-length navy cloak with the hood
  pulled up over your head*
- ♥ *wearing an astronaut's suit, a suit of armour, or
  dressing up as a gladiator or samurai warrior.*

*Feel free to chop and change the protection
visualizations you use and to experiment with your own
ideas and imagery.*

---

purchase the very best of everything to make our lives more comfortable, secure, and safe we cannot prevent suffering. Do not allow yourself to fall into the trap of believing that you can shield, protect, or even prevent problems and pain occurring.

Encouraged as we are to believe that we can exercise such control in our lives there is little wonder that when something truly catastrophic happens we are totally unprepared for it. If we aren't taught about the nature of life or equipped with the life skills to deal with it how are we supposed to be able to cope when it all goes horribly wrong?

Life is inherently contradictory; in fact its duality is perfect. There is good and bad, happy and sad, easy and hard, high and low, wonderful and hideous, joyous and sorrowful. For every positive there is a negative, and for every negative there is a positive. If you open up your heart to love, you automatically open it up to pain—it is the other side of the coin. There might be prenuptial agreements but there is no guarantee or insurance policy you can sign up to in the affairs of the heart, and there is no one who can fix your problem when your heart is broken. It is your life, your choices, and your responsibility. It is painful, hard work, and traumatic, but *heartbreak is intrinsic to life and love.* It is not easy but that is how it is.

If your heart is broken you must remember that you are not alone, you have not been picked on and singled out for misery. Heartbreak is the symbiotic counterpart to love. Accept your pain as a measure of your depth of love, accept your heartache as a worthy price for the affection and happiness you felt. Don't rail against what has happened to you and do not rage at the card life has dealt you. Focus all your energy on healing, growing, and learning everything you can from the experience then you will truly enrich yourself.

Another characteristic of life is change. Nothing in life stays the same, everything around us whether natural, man-made, animal, vegetable, or mineral is always changing, growing, evolving, adapting, and transforming; everything has its season or time of being. Given that change is such an integral element of life it is amazing to think that so many of us are threatened and frightened by it. Surely we should be used to this constant?

Instant Soother

If you need a fresh perspective on what you're thinking try this.

What advice would you give if it were someone else coming to you with this problem? What approach would you take? How sympathetic would you be? What words of wisdom would you share? Often we are far harder on ourselves than we are on our friends and loved ones. "Be as kind and compassionate to yourself as you would a dear friend."

Change is neither good nor bad, negative or positive; in fact it's not the word that is the problem, it's what the word implies that is the issue. Change means that we will have to do something differently. It means that we will have to alter, vary, modify, readjust, or amend. Our instinctive reaction when told we need to change something is to want to resist. It immediately invokes the stubborn resilient aspects within our personality—"Why should I?" "I don't want to," and ultimately "No." Change threatens the familiar, easy, security of comfort we have built and that we will go to great lengths to protect.

Practical DIY

Spring cleaning

Having a thorough spring clean can freshen and re-energize the energy in your home. Use the following suggestions to help you reclaim your territory, and symbolically cast out the old.

1. *Remove any photos, mementos, or possessions that haunt you and barb your peace of mind. Clear out your junk and in doing so clear your mind.*

2. *Have a thorough spring clean, open the windows and allow the winds of change to blow in and cleanse your room. As you clean ask the universe to help you refresh and renew the energies in your home. The smoke from burning sage also acts as a powerful cleanser.*

3. *Rearrange the room or, if you can, why not redecorate? Alternatively, treat yourself to some new accessories that will bring a fresh touch and a new splash of life and color. Pillows, drapes, artwork, throws, and duvets can make a huge difference.*

The key to the problem of change is attitude. Change has taken place in your life and the questions are: "What are you going to do about it?" and "How are you going to respond to it?" You have a choice. You can see the changes that surround you as something to be intimidated by and scared of, or you can see them as a challenge. True you might not have wanted these particular challenges you are facing to have taken place; you definitely would not have chosen a broken heart but it has happened, so resign yourself to the truth of the situation, accept the condition you are in, and embrace the challenge of change with positivity and the determination and resignation to succeed.

Change is a transition from one state of being to another; it promotes learning and wisdom, and it opens up the door of opportunity. Whether you want to admit it or not at the moment, we all need challenges in our lives. If everything was to stay the same and nothing ever change, boredom and frustration would soon set in. Change is healthy. If you can find the strength and courage to embrace the changes that have taken place in your life with positivity and determination, the universe can join forces with you and conspire to help you in all that you do. Do not hesitate

Body Balm

Flower Essence Services offers the following remedies.

♥ *For stagnation and the inability to move forward toward change try cayenne.*
♥ *For heavy-heartedness and a lack of confidence when facing difficult circumstances try borage.*
♥ *For lethargy, procrastination, and the inability to take straightforward action try tansy.*

in asking, invoking, calling, requesting, talking, or praying to the universe or God (whatever you conceive Him to be). Ask for what you need, and trust that you will receive.

We all adjust, mold, shape, blend, and compromise ourselves when we are in a relationship. When the relationship ends you don't have to do this any more. You are free to please yourself, to do what you want, when and how you choose. You don't have to compromise or give and take, you can be totally and utterly selfish. Spend some time thinking about what this liberation means to you in positive terms. What can you do now that you couldn't or wouldn't have done before?

Don't be scared by this newfound freedom. With time you will get used to the new life that is unfolding, and the old familiar patterns and routines will be replaced with new ones. Things that seem odd and strange now will become second nature more quickly than you realize.

Practical DIY

The opportunities of change

Change can be positive, liberating, exciting, and adventurous. Instead of allowing change to threaten you why not turn the tables on your fears and take the time to see what advantages change could have in store for you. What goals, dreams, hobbies, qualifications, or aspirations have you thought about but never acted on? Banish the fear of change by getting proactice, and start making your dreams come true!

Body Balm

Go out and treat yourself. Have a massage, a facial, a pedicure, or a manicure. Change your hairstyle or at least enjoy a trip to the hairdressers for a wash and blow-dry of your existing style. Buy yourself some new clothes, make-up and / or accessories to revamp your image and to help you feel good about yourself. There are some aspects to change that can be great fun.

Many people waste enormous amounts of time and energy fighting the end of their relationship. Instead of focusing their energy on recovery they become trapped in a futile circle of confusion, pain, and discord by refusing to accept the inevitable. Do not waste your precious life in this way. Accept the pain of your broken heart, come to terms with the end of your relationship, and instead of clinging to what has gone channel your energy into positive action, peace, hope, and the possibilities that lie ahead.

The path of least resistance offers you the challenge of flowing in harmony with life and the universe. It asks that you trust that everything happens for a reason and that right here, right now, at this very moment, even though you are hurting, life is still unfolding exactly as it should.

Life is hard and the path of least resistance is not an easy route, however it is the only way that you will ever find peace of mind and it is the only path to the timeless fields of love. At this difficult time do all you can to invest in your future happiness and well-being. Accept your pain with resignation, face your fears with courage, march with intent toward new doors of opportunity and possibility, and know in your heart of hearts that the universe is right beside you with every step you take.

Step 4

— ■ —

Learning Life's Lessons:
The Purpose of Pain

*A*t a time when loss is nibbling away at the edges of your being it is easy to find yourself wondering what life is really all about. What's the point of going through all this heartbreak? Why is life so hard? It might surprise you to find out that the answer to these questions is amazingly simple and can be summed up in one word: "learning." Your education did not stop when you left school or graduated from college: life is your classroom and the opportunity for learning, growing, and evolving is ever present. Each experience that you face, even the painful ones like your heartbreak, is a stepping-stone that can lead you to enlightenment and wisdom.

Body Balm

Flower Essence Services offers the following remedies.

♥ *To help you reattune to your inner voice and be true to yourself try mullein.*

♥ *To help you to see the bigger picture of life and learn your lessons try sage.*

♥ *To help promote precise thinking, clarity, and focus try mountain pennyroyal.*

As you move through the loss of a loved one it is easy to let your thoughts dwell on futile and negative issues. It does not have to be like this—you have the power to lead your thoughts. Instead of saying, "Why me?" ask yourself, "What can I learn from my heartache?" Rather than lingering on issues such as "It's not fair" or "I don't deserve this" try to explore the questions "What lessons has this experience revealed?" and "What can I learn from this horrible mess?"

By challenging what has taken place and turning a quizzical eye inward to explore, examine, and question what lessons your heartbreak can reveal, not only are you empowering yourself to find the silver lining in your cloud of pain but you are also opening the gateway to a whole new world of learning and insight. Do not be dismayed that the subject matter for your learning is your own heartbreak, the sad truth is that most of us seem to learn, evolve, and grow the most when life is hard. This is especially the case when we are hurting and when things appear to have gone awry. Unfortunately pain and hardship, not joy and happiness, tend to be our biggest teachers.

Trying to see the lessons your lost relationship can reveal has a profound effect on your entire being. Adopting an inquiring attitude creates an immediate shift in the energy of your thoughts; it also has a deep effect on your spiritual self.

Just like a tiny seed planted deep within the earth your true, eternal spirit lies deep within the center of your body. The moment you decide that you want to become a seeker of knowledge and insight, the warm glow of your intention shines down on your spirit and, very slowly and gently, it begins to unfold. As you begin to learn, understand, and grow so too does your spiritual

Practical DIY

Getting a better perspective

Smoky quartz has a quiet and calming energy. Because it is great at absorbing energy, it is highly effective at grounding the mind and the body, promoting emotional calm and mental clarity. You will need two smoky quartz crystals—try to buy two that have naturally occurring points or terminations to one end so that the energy can be naturally directed.

1. *Lie down on your bed or on the floor, with your legs slightly parted. Place one of the crystals in the base of your throat in the dip where you can feel the knobbly edges of your collarbones meeting your breastbone. Make sure the point of the crystal is facing downward toward your feet.*

2. *Place the second crystal between your knees, once again making sure that its point faces toward your feet. Relax and stay in this position with the crystals for at least 5 minutes.*

self. In this way the riches of spirit are learned and the light that shines on your spirit is a true reflection of all that you have experienced. Your true spiritual self forms the very fabric of your being. Lying deep within you it can be glimpsed through the sparkle in your eyes, the glow of energy in your presence, and the love, compassion, and kindness radiating out from your heart.

Body Balm

The electromagnetic energy field that surrounds your body is called the aura.
Your aura can get clogged up with unwanted negative energy. To cleanse and refresh it, simply sprinkle sea salt in your bath water. Try this twice a week and you will ensure your aura is in tip-top shape.

Whether you feel devastated that the relationship is over, angry that you ever got involved, frustrated that you wasted your time, or you are struggling with the aftermath of a destructive relationship, try to see the experience as an opportunity for growth and learning. Gather your strength and summon up your courage to peer into the past, analyze what happened, and see what lessons you can find that can make you stronger and wiser. This is your chance to use your grief as a springboard for knowledge, insight, and personal development.

If you wish to turn your heartache into wisdom you need to be prepared to reflect on the relationship you have lost. You will need to ponder lots of different issues and questions, some of which might be painful. Only you can decide when you are ready to do this; only you know when you have got to a place where this will be possible. Be patient with yourself and do not rush, listen to your intuition and what feels right. If you are still in the deep turmoil of emotional pain then quite clearly you are not ready to look dispassionately at what took place. If, however, you have put the raw pain of emotion behind you and are settling down into your new routine of life then perhaps you are indeed in a good space to start reflecting on the lessons you can learn. If you find that it gets too much you can always stop and return to reflect some other time. This process is meant to help enlighten you, not to add to your burden. Do not be a harsh taskmaster on yourself.

When you feel you are ready to begin, start by looking at the relationship that has just ended and ask yourself what lessons you can learn from it. Be objective,

Picture This

Being grounded

In order to have a balanced outlook you need to be balanced. When you are off-kilter it will be impossible to make level, sensible, and grounded decisions. Creative visualization exercises are an ideal way of grounding.

Sit down and close your eyes. Relax by following the gentle flow of your breath. When you are ready, imagine that you have a large root growing from the bottom of each of your feet (if you don't like the idea of roots you can use cords or ribbons).

Visualize your roots burrowing downward through the ground and into the dark, rich soil below. Continue visualizing their growth until you are securely anchored in the core of the earth. When you feel firmly rooted, spend a few minutes experiencing what it is like to be grounded, anchored, and balanced. You can take the visualization one step further by imagining the energy of the earth traveling up through your roots and into your body. You can picture the energy as a color, electricity, or even sparkling lights. When you are ready and feel fully re-energized, open your eyes and bring your full consciousness back into the room you are in.

rational, and as impartial as possible, and try to look at it from every angle. As you do this you might like to write down your thoughts and feelings—putting pen to paper is both cathartic and clarifying.

By looking at the strengths and weaknesses of the relationship you will have a good perspective on the whole affair. No matter how wonderful or hideous the relationship was, you can learn from what took place. Do not allow yourself to get negative—if you have learnt, grown, and discovered then the experience has been invaluable in spite of the pain and heartache suffered. More often than not, the most painful moments in our life turn out to be the most valuable. Try to remain detached from the conclusions that arise. This is not an exercise in creating guilt and remorse or apportioning blame. The purpose is to look and see what you can learn from the experience.

Use the information that emerges to manifest change in your life; aim to build on your strengths and strengthen your weaknesses. By doing this, not only will you enhance your recovery, health, and wisdom, you will also ensure that your future relationships are far healthier and happier.

Practical DIY

Taking stock

The following questions are all designed to help you reflect upon the relationship that has just ended. The key is to stay detached, concentrating your energies on what you can learn.

♥ *What were the strengths—what worked? What was great, comfortable, suitable, and right about it?*

♥ *What were the weaknesses? What caused problems, upsets, arguments, and disagreements?*

♥ *What went wrong? Where and why did the relationship fail?*

♥ *What has this relationship shown you? What lessons can you learn from it? What positives can be drawn from the experience?*

♥ *If you could go back and do it all over again what would you change? What would you do differently?*

Do not forget that you have the power to change anything you don't like. You can re-write any unwanted patterns and programs of behavior. As in Step 3 you can do this through affirmations and creative visualizations or, if you feel you need the input of a professional, you can seek the help of a Neuro Linguistic Practitioner, a counsellor, or a therapist. You have the power at your disposal to heal your pain, resculpt your life and change your future experience(s) of love.

When you are ready to explore your love life lessons, you can begin to look at the person that you chose to love. What was your ex like? Were they suitable for you? Did they fulfill your needs and have the traits that you would choose if you were asked to describe your ideal partner? Often we can be quite specific in the type of person that would best suit us and then we go out and begin dating someone totally mismatched to our needs.

Try the character profile exercise in the "Practical DIY" box to build up a clear picture of your own character profile versus that of your ex. Knowledge is power and by questioning, probing, and explaining, you will equip yourself with all the information you need to get a better insight into the relationship that just broke your heart.

It can also be very informative to look at all the previous relationships that you have had. Take time to reflect

Practical DIY

Character Profiles

Sometimes it's easier to see things when they are written out in front of you. The following exercise is a great way to explore just how compatible you and your ex really were.

PART A

Write a profile of yourself—what kind of person are you? Be honest about all your good and not so good points. You might consider words like friendly, moody, optimistic, stubborn, etc.

What makes you happy? What makes you laugh and smile? What makes life worth living? What do you enjoy? What are your hobbies and passions? What brings out the best in you? What enriches your world? When you have finished, put away your profile for at least a week before moving on to Part B.

PART B

Now go through all the same points in relation to your ex. When you have finished compare the two profiles. Just how compatible were you and your ex? What conclusions can you draw from this exercise?

on your love affairs and your relationship history. Have you gone for different types of people or have you gone for the same "type" of person over and over again? Do your ex-partners all fit into the same mold? Do they have any similar traits and patterns of behavior? Do you think that you have done a good job in picking the right partners, or have you gone from one unsuccessful relationship to another? Do the same issues, problems, or types of personality keep recurring?

Instant Soother

Boji stones are great at helping to enhance vitality, balance, optimism, and courage. They are believed to accelerate healing, and have a beneficial influence on blood, circulation, and the immune system. They are also great at helping to ground. They come in pairs, and all you need to do is hold the male stone in your left hand and the female stone in your right hand to bring about mental and emotional harmony and promote general healing. They can be bought on the Internet and at some New Age shops.

Body Balm

Smoothies are a quick and nutritious way to enjoy fruit and vegetables. They make an ideal breakfast if you are off your food or can't be bothered to cook anything. Combine the fruit of your choice with a splash of fruit juice, milk, or yoghurt and enjoy experimenting with your food blender / liquidizer. Mix blueberries with blackberries, peaches with strawberries—even banana and blueberry is delicious. Add milk if the mixture is too thick, a drizzle of honey if it's too sharp, or a small handful of ice cubes if you fancy an iced drink. You can't go wrong!

If you want to review the possible similarities and differences between your ex-partners try writing out a character profile as in Practical DIY page 73 for each person, making sure that you include their character and behavior traits, as well as their strengths and weaknesses. When you have finished compare the character profiles and see if anything interesting reveals itself.

If you can see any particular trends or patterns taking place congratulate yourself: you have reached an amazing life-changing moment. Only when you can see that a pattern exists can you change it, and only when you change that pattern can you free yourself of it and move forward, empowered and liberated, into a new dawn of life and love.

Another point that you might like to consider is the similarities that can exist between you, your ex-partners and your parents. Are all or any of your ex-partners just like your parent(s)? For example, if you have grown up with a father who bullied and dominated the family you might find that you have picked lovers who behaved the same way. If you have grown up with cold and unloving parents then you might find that you are drawn to cold and inexpressive partners, or that you find it hard to express your emotions.

Alternatively, it might be you mimicking the behaviour of one of your parents. You might be sacrificing your own needs for these of your partners in just the same way your mother always puts your father first. Once again, you can use character profiles to compare and contrast you, your parents and your ex-partner(s). Pay close attention to any patterns that emerge. Ask yourself what conclusions might be drawn from the information that is emerging.

Body Balm

Don't be lonely—get active. Join a group, club, or society. Begin an evening class. Take up a social hobby—one where you will meet people. Join a health club or a gym. Buy a pet, offer your time to voluntary work. Go to group therapy. Get a part-time job. Expand your horizons.

Most of us go about our adult lives running through the same scripts that we learnt as children. In just the same way as you etched the alphabet deep into your subconscious mind, you also set down hundreds of patterns of behavior and hundreds of learned responses. The patterns you learnt as a child are deeply entrenched in your being and, without you knowing, still shape your view of the world and influence your behavior, decisions, choices, and responses every single day of your life. If, after careful consideration, you feel that certain unwanted patterns are recurring, then you can seek the help of a professional therapist to liberate yourself from them.

While the end of a relationship is a painful and lonely time, it does force your hand to start again. Whether you like it or not you have a new beginning—a clean slate. Be reflective and spend some time thinking about

---

Picture This

A new day, a fresh start

Dawn symbolizes new beginnings and new opportunities. Try this beautiful creative visualization to open the door to the wonder, beauty, and magic each new day can bring you.

Sit down and close your eyes. Relax by following the gentle flow of your breath. When you are ready, visualize a beautiful new day dawning. Make it as real as possible by adding as much detail as you can—sounds, smells, touch, feelings, emotions. Now begin to walk toward that new dawn and immerse yourself in it, enjoying the wonder, and beauty. Stay in the beautiful light for as long as you want.

---

where you would like your life to go from here. Instead of seeing your life in terms of shattered dreams and a broken heart, lift your eyes to the horizon of what lies ahead and what you would like the future to hold. Never forget that what you set your mind to is what you manifest in your life. Visualize your dreams coming true and manifest the future that you want.

What kind of person would you like to attact into your life? With the benefit of hindsight, what do you now know that will help you make better choices in your future love life?

Ask yourself questions and get informed. What works for you in a relationship? What doesn't? What are you happy to tolerate? What and where are your boundary lines? What will you no longer tolerate? What are you happy to accept and compromise over? What are your expectations and hopes?

The better you know yourself the more discerning and appropriate life choices you will be able to make. You will only ever be able to effectively filter the winners and losers of any possible future romantic liaisons if you can measure their compatibility to you, and you

Practical DIY

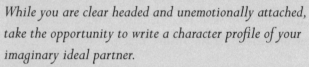

An ideal match

PART A

While you are clear headed and unemotionally attached, take the opportunity to write a character profile of your imaginary ideal partner.

Consider what personality, values, belief systems, traits, temperament, interests, background, and lifestyle, they would have. You could be realistic and grade this as must-haves, should-haves and could-haves.

PART B

Write a "relationship mission statement" outlining what kind of relationship you wish to have. Build your mission statement on what defines compatible harmonies, happy, and fulfilled to you.

When you begin dating again, before you allow yourself to be swept up in the excitement of a second, third or fourth date, pause for thought. Read your character profile and mission statement. No one will tick all your boxes in Part A but do they tick enough to interest you? Do they tick enough to start the relationship off in the right direction? Are they worthy of your love? Are they compatible with you and your mission statement?

can only measure their compatibility by knowing your-self and what you want. This isn't about establishing guarantees—love is more often than not always a gamble, there is *no* Mr or Ms Perfect, and any relationship is a delicate balance of give, take and compromise.

This is about putting yourself in the best possible position to make informed, healthy, and positive decisions about your love life and who you choose to let into your heart.

When a relationship ends our minds are often filled with questions, most of all "Why?" But all too often we tend to stop short of the really searching questions that would be of greater value to us. The more honest you can be with yourself, and the further you are prepared to delve and explore your heartbreak, the more enlightened you will become and the easier it will be to heal your heart and come to terms with your loss.

Heartbreak cracks open complacency and normality, and challenges you to take a fresh look at yourself and your life. It offers you the chance of beginning a journey of self-discovery. The very thing that hurts you can be the catalyst to great personal transformation and enlightenment; sometimes it can be a blessing in disguise. The knowledge you gain from your experience and your questions will empower you with insight and self-awareness. You will be able to step forward confident that you have the wisdom and understanding to make healthy and positive life choices, and to select future partners who will complement and enhance your life.

You will be able to replace anger with understanding, sadness with insight, resentment with acceptance. You will be able to see that through the sacrifice of a broken heart you gained priceless knowledge and wisdom. You will understand why the ancient sages have always preached that heartbreak is man's greatest teacher and why love is at the heart of mankind's spiritual evolution. When heartbreak hasn't been pointless, when you can see the bigger picture, understand the lessons and insights your heartbreak has revealed and turned despair and pain into knowledge, you will have reached a truly inspirational turning point in your life. By turning your pain around in this way a whole new world of possibility awaits you, and your life, for all the right reasons will never be the same again.

Step 5
— ∎ —

Discovering the Power Within:
A Whole New You

Starting to accept the changes that have taken place in your life and becoming aware of the lessons that have revealed themselves in your heartache are sure signs that you are well on the way to mending your broken heart. As a result of your endeavors you have set yourself on the path to recovery and well-being. But what if there was a wealth of potential lying dormant within you that could enhance your recovery and transform your quality of life? Discover the power within and allow a whole new dimension of your being to unfold by embracing your true spiritual self.

Many people are unaware that they have a spiritual dimension, yet your spirit is the absolute essence of who you are. It is your greatest asset and your most priceless possession, and when it comes to facing the challenge of recovering from a broken heart it is your most valuable resource.

Instant Soother

The energy of certain crystals can enhance your spiritual work.

♥ *For promoting spiritual attunement try azurite or turquoise.*
♥ *For spiritual awakening try lapis lazuli or celestine.*
♥ *For integration of the earthly self with the spiritual self try fluorite.*

To begin unlocking the power that lies within your spirit all you need to do is open the door of curiosity. The wonderful thing about your spirit is that it responds very quickly to the energy of your desire and intent. The second you begin to wonder about this invisible and divine facet of your being the energy of your thoughts begins to nurture your spirit and it starts to unfold.

The easiest way of picturing your spirit is to imagine that you have a candle burning inside your heart. When you become so consumed in the material aspects of life and live in ignorance of your spiritual self the candle burns a low, tiny flame; when you embrace your spiritual self your flame burns brightly and shines with such a radiance that its emanates out through your physical body. Others are instinctively drawn to this lovely glowing energy and want to be near you.

Your spiritual body is composed of two elements—your spirit and your soul. Although they are very similar and inextricably linked there is a subtle difference between them. Your spirit is of heavenly extraction; it is the connection you have with the universe; it is the divine essence that interconnects you to everything and everyone.

Your spirit manifests itself through the delicate and fine mental and emotional bodies of your soul. In this way your soul acts as a sort of mediator between your spirit and your body. Your soul is what makes you who you

Picture This

The flame within

This gentle creative visualization enables you to begin to connect with your spirit. As the energy of your thoughts blends with the essence of your being your spirit will begin to unfold and blossom, and you will open the door to the magic within you and the wonder of connection and communication.

Sit down and close your eyes. Relax by following the gentle flow of your breath. When you are ready, look down with your mind's eye into your heart and see the candle of your spiritual flame burning. Energy follows thought so as you focus your awareness on your spiritual self notice the flame of the candle growing in size and brightness. Watch the flame intensifying so that its light shines through every cell and fiber of your body. Connect with this energy and feel it restoring, replenishing, and enriching you physically, emotionally, mentally, and spiritually. Bask in this light for as long as is comfortable and repeat the exercise as often as you like.

are—it is your mind, will, intellect, and emotions. In this way your spirit and your soul blend together to form your spiritual self.

Body Balm

Deep relaxation enables you to disconnect from your body and reach a deeper spiritual level. Try lying down flat on the floor/bed. Starting with your toes and feet, work your way up through all the muscle groups in your body, tightening and clenching the muscles then relaxing them. When you reach your head, lie still for a further 5 minutes and enjoy the feeling of relaxation within your entire body.

Your spirit talks to you through the still, small voice within. It is the voice of intuition that can help to guide, advise, and direct you, not just as you work to cleanse and heal your heart but as you move onward with your life. On many occasions throughout your life you will already have heard this voice; it is speaking to you whenever you get a "gut feeling" or a "hunch." It is that innate sense of knowing; it is what we are referring to when we say "I knew I shouldn't have done that." Maybe, deep down, you even knew that your ex was going to be trouble.

Picture This

Touching the stillness within

We are constantly bombarded by external stimuli, whether it is the TV, the radio, or our families. Yet silent time is enriching, invigorating, and restorative. Try to set aside time to be still and quiet.

Sit down and close your eyes. Relax by following the gentle flow of your breath. When you are ready, light a candle and settle down in front of it in a comfortable chair. Focus your thoughts upon the flame and allow all other thoughts to fall away. You can continue staring at the candle and use it as a focus, or you can close your eyes and allow yourself to "just be." If other thoughts begin to encroach, open your eyes again and refocus on the candle or visualize the candle in your mind's eye. Try to sit like this for 5–15 minutes as regularly as possible—daily if you can. With time and practice, this exercise will become easier.

Your spiritual body is your antenna into the world: it knows what's best for you and if you want to make the right life decisions you must be in tune with it. The trouble is that most of the time we rarely get the chance to hear this innate wisdom because everything else drowns it out. Whether it is the constant chatter of your mind, a busy working environment, people, family, the radio, the television, or the phone, we seldom seem to find ourselves free of external stimuli. If you want to commune with your spirit and open up the channels of communication with it, you need to shut out the clamor of your busy world and all its noisy distractions.

Whenever you set aside time to be still and silent you are creating the space within which your spiritual voice can be heard. With practice and experience you will be able to hear, sense, and feel its guidance and, empowered by your inner wisdom, you will be able to step forward with greater confidence. Next time love bobs its head up on the horizon you will be able to draw on your intuition to help you decide if this person "feels" right. Go within, and see if you get a sense, feeling, hunch, or instinct, and listen to whatever you get. You will be able to make all your life decisions and choices safe in the knowledge that you are doing the right thing.

When you listen to the voice of intuition and go with what "feels right" and comfortable, you flow in accordance with the universe and your own unique destiny. When you go against your intuition you often get a sense that what you're doing "doesn't quite sit right"—it will feel wrong or uncomfortable. The more you get to experience these two different senses the more quickly you will be able to make the right choice. It is more than likely that there will be times when you choose to ignore what your intuition tells you—but, remember, it is never too late to admit you made the wrong choice and do something about it.

People spend years searching for truth, meaning, and answers in the world around them. The irony is that everything that you will ever need is right inside of you. You already have all the answers and signposts. Right at this very minute, as you are gathering strength and healing your heartbreak, turn to your inner spirit for strength, power, and direction.

When getting over the breakup of a relationship there will, of course, be good days and bad days. Like waves crashing against the shore you will find different thoughts and feelings washing over you. The more regularly that you can be still and find the peace within, the more balanced and peaceful you will become. Nurturing your spiritual connection will help to ground you and bring you greater emotional and mental stability. You will get more joy out of the good days and, when you feel low, have a bad day, or turmoil presents itself again you will find yourself better anchored to ride out the storms. Nurturing your spirit will make you stronger and shore up the foundations of your being.

Instant Soother

The vibrations of classical music have a very uplifting and profound effect on the spirit. Enjoy this music as a soothing backdrop to your life, and give your spiritual body the space to reach out and grow.

All that you experience as you walk your path of life touches your mind, body, and spirit. During the times when your heartbreak caused you chaos, your body might have been tense, weary, and stressed, your mind

Picture This

Lift your spirits

Even if you have set yourself firmly on the path to recovery, there are still likely to be days when you feel flat, sad, or lost. Try this uplifting creative visualization to help you through the low periods.

Sit down and close your eyes. Relax by following the gentle flow of your breath. When you are ready, imagine that you are standing in front of a beautiful rainbow. As you gaze at it you realize that it has a flight of stairs ascending toward and into it. Climb up the stairs into the rainbow until you reach its very heart. Sit down and watch all the colors swirling around you and enveloping you. Visualize these beautiful colors penetrating every fiber of your being so that any negative and dark thoughts and feelings inside you become transformed with color until you are glowing like the rainbow. Remain there for as long as you want. When you are ready, stand up, and walk back down the stairs and out of the rainbow.

might have been in torment, and your emotions shattered, but your spirit shone. Now that you realize it
exists, never stop believing in the celestial power of
your spirit. It might be invisible and intangible but your
spirit is indestructible: it is the divine spark of creation
that connects you to the universe, the people, and the
world in which you live.

Every time you empty and clear your mind the spiritual
self is able to surface and find expression. The more you
practice being still and connecting with your spiritual
self, the easier it will become to tune in to and link with
it. As your spiritual self blossoms and unfolds, so too
will your insight, sensitivity, and awareness. You will
begin to feel differently. A new, enlightened, perspective on your relationship with your ex will emerge.
Threads of confidence will weave into the fabric of
your being. A sense of calm and peace will radiate out
from your soul, and the pain of your heartbreak will be
smoothed over with love and well-being.

As you nurture your strength of spirit you will develop
an empowering connection with the real inner you, the
person beneath the persona you have created on the
outside. In touch with who you really are, you will be

able to delve into ever greater depths of personal insight and learning. You will discover amazing things about yourself and what you are capable of achieving.

As you begin to unfold and connect with your spirit you will find that along with insight, wisdom and inner strength your compassion, forgiveness and love may also start to change and evolve. A gentle purifying process starts on every level of your being and often layers of pain gently emerge. Using the various tools and techniques on offer in "Body Balm," "Instant Soother" and "Picture This" you have at your disposal all

---

Body Balm

You can enjoy using flower remedies to support your spiritual endeavors.

♥ *To enhance your ability to listen to your intuition, as well as helping you to open up to inspiration, try using olive (Bach).*

♥ *For open and expansive spirituality, and to enhance meditative insight try violet (Flower Essence Services).*

Instant Soother

Use frankincense, jasmine, and lotus essential oils as a perfume or air freshener to enhance your spirituality and your spiritual awareness. Enjoy peace and relaxation in a bath that has had a few drops of orange blossom mixed into the water. Sprinkle a few drops of chamomile on your pillow to aid restful sleep.

you need to deal with this and ensure that even your deepest wounds and scars are healed. Never underestimate the power of love in being able to mend your broken heart or bringing miracles into your life.

Nurturing your spirit will also nurture strength, courage, and wisdom, and you will begin to see for yourself how the chaos of heartbreak has been the catalyst for change. New perspectives of understanding will help you to get more out of your life. As the divine within you blossoms, you will attract divine things to you. Blessings, miracles, coincidences, and universal moments will bring magic to your life and a smile to your face.

Picture This

Ripples in the pond

The following creative visualization is a wonderful way to clear your mind of thoughts and to touch the stillness within. Sit down and close your eyes. Relax by following the gentle flow of your breath. When you are ready, visualize yourself standing in front of a beautiful pond on which a boat is being blown about in the wind. Its motion is causing the surface of the pond to be filled with ripples. Watch as the ripples of water roll out from the boat in concentric circles until they splash against the shoreline. Reach out with your mind's eye and steady the boat so that the ripples gently subside and the surface of the water becomes a perfectly smooth reflective surface. Note how still everything becomes, and allow yourself to become absorbed in the tranquility. Stay by the pond as long as you feel comfortable.

Nurturing your spirit will open up the gateway to your higher consciousness and the universe. Once you welcome the universe into your life you can be sure that it will become enriched. The universe will be able to see the light of your spirit and will be drawn toward you.

As you strive ahead, the universe will conspire to help you in all you do.

Your awareness and sensitivities will also unfold. You will become more sensitive to the people, places, and situations that you find yourself in. You will be able to sense and feel whether things are right or wrong, and you will be able to depend on your own judgment, especially when it comes to picking a suitable person to date. You won't make silly errors of judgment because you will be able to look within and sense what is the right thing to do.

Your spiritual self is eternal and divine. Fan its flames with your awareness and your spirit will unfold, and as it does so it will shine like a radiant light from deep

---

Instant Soother

Next time you have a problem write it down on a piece of paper. Tuck this under your pillow and literally "sleep on it." The very first thought, feeling, or sense that comes to you in the morning is your intuitive answer to the problem.

within you. You will be able to carve yourself a new beginning where personal power, insight, and wisdom are your guiding strengths. Secure, strong, and confident, at one with every dimension of your being, and in tune with your spiritual self, you will flow in harmony with the universe.

All the pain, heartache, grief, and sadness of your lost love will transform into greater self-understanding that manifests itself in your life as genuine peace, well-being, happiness, and fulfillment. You won't just recover from your broken heart, you will be able to turn your personal tragedy into the most profound and enlightening journey of discovery, knowledge, growth, and success.

Step 6

— ∎ —

Beginning the Rest of your Life: A New Dawn

*W*hether it happens consciously or unconsciously, there comes a point along the road to healing when you emerge from the dark tunnel of pain and despair into the light. You might not know when it happened but you come to realize that the good days far outweigh the bad and that, at long last, life is finally OK again.

Welcome to the new chapter of your life and a new dawn of beginnings. Doesn't it feel great? But before you sit back and breathe a sigh of relief that the worst is behind you, you might like to consider whether your journey has come to an end.

Instant Soother

Every day make sure that you notice something beautiful. Whether it is a fabulous smile, a glorious sunset, or a child's laugh, there is joy and wonder to behold if you are prepared to see. The more you search for beautiful things the more beautiful the world will be.

Over the past five steps you have discovered how to mend your heart as well as the triumph that can emerge from pain. You have got to know yourself on a new level, and you have discovered resilience, strength, and fortitude. You have learnt a great deal about yourself and gained insight into the life choices you have made. You have just begun to discover the power within and the wonder and magic that spirituality can bring to your life. Now that you have come this far can you really just stop? Or would you like to continue evolving and growing, and carry on with your exciting journey?

Let *Six Spiritual Steps to Mend a Broken Heart* share with you the six spiritual truths that will enable you to continue forward on your journey of recovery and personal transformation. The simple spiritual philosophy contained within these pages can show you how to sculpt your attitudes and approach to life so that you can continue healing your heart as well as finding even greater happiness, contentment, and purpose in your day-to-day existence.

1. Attitude

As you have worked through the steps in this book, you will have learnt how the attitudes that you have form the filter through which you view life. If you have a negative outlook then not only will you perceive the world as a negative place but your experience of life will also be negative. Likewise, if you have a positive disposition then the world and your experience of it will be positive. Having an attitude that enables you to enjoy and value life is critical if you want to feel happy, fulfilled, and contented. Choose to remain optimistic about your heartbreak and about the life that lies ahead.

As discussed in Step 3, not only do your thoughts affect the health of your body, they also play a major role in sending out clear signals of intent and desire to the sub-conscious mind and the universe. Be careful what you wish for because it just might happen!

In the days and weeks ahead, continue to pay attention to the thoughts that you dwell on and, as far as possible, refuse to allow negative thoughts to creep in. Choose to see everything that has taken place in positive terms. Don't succumb to futile regrets or the nagging thoughts of hindsight. Strive to focus on constructive, positive, and happy thoughts, and you will quickly see positive changes manifesting in every aspect of your life. Remember the law of attraction and the path of resistance? What you give you get back, and what you resist persists. What you want to have in your life you must give. Go with the flow and foster strength as well as flexibility of spirit.

Strive to maintain a childlike simplicity in your out-look. As we grow up we learn the complexities of life and, at the same time, make life overcomplicated. Children have a very accepting, flexible approach to life; they adapt well to situations and appreciate the small things. Try to adopt this outlook to get the most out of every moment.

Practical DIY

Mindfulness

Mindfulness is a form of active meditation that requires you to give your full and undivided attention to what you're doing—your mind is not allowed to wander off and start thinking of other things. It requires lots of practice for the mind is not used to being disciplined, but if you persevere you can improve your concentration and gain mastery over your thoughts. It also helps you to practice getting the most out of every moment. Here are just some of the moments when you could apply mindfulness in your day-to-day life:

♥ *chores*
♥ *washing-up*
♥ *making and drinking a coffee/tea*
♥ *eating*
♥ *gardening*
♥ *listening to music*

♥ *walking, driving, or cycling*
♥ *preparing and cooking a meal*
♥ *taking a bath or a shower*
♥ *washing and cleaning the car*
♥ *listening to and conversing with others.*

Be realistic about the world in which you live. Pain exists and, from time to time, it ensnares us all in its vice-like grip; however, there is also much joy and pleasure to be had. Be pragmatic in your attitude toward pain but never give up on love, for in the ever changing seasons of the earth, love is perennial.

2. Love

Love is the most powerful energy that exists. Love can conquer all; it nurtures the mind, the body, and the spirit; it can heal the deepest wounds, and vanquish anger, bitterness, enmity, and evil. Love is the greatest tool at your disposal for healing and it lies at the heart of enjoying a rich and meaningful life. It is the most important center of your being, from which you can live and work.

Defining love is quite difficult; however, in the Bible (Corinthians 1, 13:4–7), there is one very beautiful verse that is a wonderful testimony to the ideal of what true love is. It says the following things: love is patient and kind, it does not envy or boast, it is not proud, rude, self-seeking, or easily angered. It does not keep records of wrongdoing and it does not delight in evil.

Love rejoices in truth, it protects, trusts, hopes, and always perseveres. There is no greater accolade to love than this. Remember these principles for love and use them as a marker for the love you give and the love you receive, and you will not go wrong.

No matter how wounded you have been, or how much love has come to hurt you, you can always choose to open your heart and let your love flow. Your heart responds immediately to your intentions so the more you think about and practice giving of your love the easier you will find it.

There are many different aspects to love: caring, compassion, charity, unpossessiveness, forgiveness, kindness, tolerance, and tenderness are just a few. In many ways love is just as varied, magical, and beautiful as a rainbow—it too has many different vibrations, shades, and colors of expression. Take time to notice the different vibrations of love that you give and receive in your life, and that you radiate outward into the world.

Set yourself the challenge of bringing more love into your life, and begin with yourself. Do not berate, chastise, belittle or ridicule yourself. Treat yourself with

Practical DIY

Self-love

Self-love is not about being vain or conceited: it is to do with having self-respect, appreciating yourself, and being good to yourself. It is valuing your strengths and being compassionate about your weaknesses. Every day strive to do the following:

♥ *treat yourself with respect*
♥ *be who you are and be positive about yourself*
♥ *be positive about the role that you play in life and the work that you do*
♥ *smile, inwardly and outwardly*
♥ *send your spirit some loving positive energy*
♥ *allow your heart to give its love.*

If you struggle with the notion of self-love then start with the possibility of being open to the idea of self-love or just being happy with who you are.

respect, value your strengths and the unique gifts and skills that you have, replace criticism and judgment with acceptance, and swap harshness for love. Be compassionate and kind to yourself. Lack of self-worth and confidence is a sign that you need to work on self-love, not so that you become vain, arrogant and big headed, but so that you can stand strong and tall with pride. Confidence and self-acceptance are key. Look out on the world with twinkling eyes and move forward with a definite spring in your step.

Once you have begun working on yourself on the issue of love and self-worth you can begin to turn your thoughts outwards. Continue working with forgiveness on those who have hurt you, including your ex. Be compassionate and forgiving in all that you see and do. Enjoy exploring the miraculous power that love has to offer and see how it can transform your life.

There are many different types of love and all of them are wonderful, but there is one type of love that is not very healthy: it is the love given on conditions. Conditional love should be titled "empty love." If love is given to you ensnared with restrictions, clauses, or expectations it lacks the very qualities that define love. Conditional love is hollow and being seen as such it should be avoided where at all possible.

The depth to which you can extend love to others is a mirror of the depth to which you can be loved yourself. Work at loosening the chains of expectation that bind your love and instead give your love unconditionally.

Forgiving others when they have broken your heart or hurt your feelings is the only way that you will heal. Forgiveness is an aspect of love that can liberate you from the wounds and scars of life. Without forgiveness there can be no recovery. The greatest gift you have in dealing with those who have hurt you or those who have shown themselves to be enemies is to forgive them. This does not mean that you go over and hug them or lay yourself open to further abuse or pain, rather it means working within you on the vibration of love and forgiveness.

They need never even know that you are exercising forgiveness and compassion, but you will create a shift in the energetic connection that exists between you both. If, for whatever reason, you can't find it in your heart to work with your ex on the vibration of forgiveness or love, you can link with the universe and visualize the unconditional love of heaven healing you both.

Love makes the world go round and if you begin to explore this omnipotent power you will open up your heart to wonderful possibilities. Your wounds will disappear and, in their place, your spirit will shine, your heart will grow, and your connection to the universe will blossom.

Practical DIY

A wish collage

Many of us have dreams, aspirations, and goals that we would like to achieve. Successful people put their energy, intent, and focus into making their dreams happen. You can start making your dreams come true by putting them down on paper or by making a "wish collage." Fill an A4, A3, or even an A2 piece of paper with pictures, images, words, and samples of everything that you aspire to and dream of. Pin this somewhere private, such as the inside of your wardrobe, and remind yourself each day of what the future can offer you and what you want to work toward.

3. Realizing your potential

From the twinkling starry night sky to the first green shoots of spring popping through the soil, the wonder of the universe is ever present. But this amazing world is not just around you: you are part of this magic too. The eternal spirit that shines within your being is the divine spark of creation that lives within all things. No matter how humble your existence you belong on this planet, you have a right to be here, and you have your own unique gifts to offer.

When we look at famous people, powerful business-men, illustrious leaders, and the brilliant minds that walk this planet, our own life can appear very drab, dull, and insignificant. It is easy for us to believe that our lives lack meaning and purpose. This is not the case, and there are two reasons why.

First, in the divine plan of the universe you too play a crucial role. Whether you realize it or not, at this very minute, you are playing an integral part in the Great Scheme of Life. By choosing to mend your broken heart by embracing simple spiritual concepts, your energy and love is also helping the universe to raise the

Practical DIY

Your unique gift

The gifts that you can bring to this world can be found in those things that you are naturally good at, or those things that you dream of doing. We sometimes overlook our gifts, thinking that everybody can do them, but often this is not the case. Here are a few ways in which you can realize the gifts you have to offer.

♥ *What are you good at? What are your strengths? What are you gifted at? What comes naturally to you?*

♥ *Ask your friends where they think your strengths lie.*

♥ *You might also find clues in your childhood. What were you naturally good at? What fascinated you? What were your dreams?*

♥ *Spend some time in quiet contemplation with your spirit about your life purpose and what would bring greater value and meaning to your life.*

♥ *Ask your higher consciousness and the universe to show you your path. Ask for the inspiration to see the gifts you can bring to this world. Really listen for the answers. They will come.*

vibration of the earth and lead mankind toward a brighter and more loving future. The second reason why your life is important is because of the unique life purpose you have come to earth to fulfill. Each and every single one of us, including you, has a special purpose for being here and special gifts to offer.

Why not turn your heartache around and, as well as healing your heart, take this new beginning as an opportunity to explore the special gifts that you have to offer?

If you have a particular talent for something, a dream burning in your heart, a secret ambition or a gut feeling that draws you toward something in particular, it is probably more than just a whim. Our talents and dreams are often the signposts to the gifts that we can give the world and the higher purpose for our journey on the planet.

If you do not yet know what your life's purpose is then either the time is not ready for you to know or you have not stopped in the stillness long enough to hear the voice of your soul. Only by going within and tapping in to your spiritual heart will you be able to connect with your divine path.

No matter what form your gift(s), talent(s), or inspiration(s) take, no matter how simple, grand, small, or large, sharing it/them with the world and bringing it/them into the fullest expression of reality, will give your life purpose. Stop dreaming about what would be fantastic, and start doing it!

4. Vision and belief

Life is best approached with inspirational vision and dogged persistence. You need to have dreams, goals, and aspirations but you cannot stop there. You also need to put energy and commitment into making them come true, and you need to believe that your dreams can become a reality.

Those people who have really made it big have done so just as much through hard work and self-belief as luck. If you can combine vision with effort, action, and belief with then you will create a really powerful force for success.

As you go about your day-to-day life never forget to ask the universe for help. Whether you need some help to keep your courage up, or to keep on going in your

Picture This

Making it happen

Together with the universe you can achieve anything you set your mind to. Whatever you would like to achieve, no matter how big or small, needs to start with the seeds of inspiration. Once you realize what you need to do you can start making it happen by visualizing your success. For example, if you would like to own a shop visualize yourself standing in it on the first morning it opens. If you want to write a book visualize yourself at your book launch party. If you want to go back to college and study, visualize yourself graduating. Believe, believe, believe! What you think you create. Your future is a product of the thoughts you think today. Get creative and start energizing your hopes and dreams with the vision of seeing them happen. Daydream them, visualize them, think them, anticipate them, and trust that the universe will help you to make them come true.

healing in order to bring your temper down, the universe can be a constant source of power and support in your life. So long as your intent is heartfelt and genuine you will always receive that which you need.

The universe can also help you to realize your dreams and ambitions. If you want something and it is appropriate that you have it, if it is meant to be yours by divine right, then the universe will conspire to help you in every way possible. If it is not meant for you it simply won't happen. Other events will occur and change your path, taking you off in another direction. Spend time with your spiritual self and you will soon be able to tell what belongs to you by divine right rather than what you merely fancy.

"Ask and you will receive, seek and you will find, knock and it will be opened for you." These are the words in the Bible (Matthew 7:7) which tell us that anything is possible to those who are willing to call, ask, and pray for the help, guidance, and support of the universe. The universe won't rummage through the muddied waters of your mind to sort the wheat from the chaff; it cannot interfere in your life and get involved without you asking; it can't open the door of opportunity if you never get off the couch. You have to put the work in too. Take the fresh start that you have been given to begin dreaming, and ask the universe for help in all that you do and all that you would like to achieve, and together you will find that anything is possible.

Instant soother

*Imagine that your problem is an
object. Put it down and step back.
Keep stepping back and, as you do so, watch your object
get smaller and smaller, less and less significant. If you
like, take flight and soar up into the air. Notice how tiny
your problem looks now, how insignificant in the scale of
creation.*

5. Detachment

Sometimes it's more of an issue of altitude than attitude. As we struggle through the challenges of life,
detachment is a great life skill to have at your disposal. While it is very difficult to practice detachment in the midst of heartbreak, now that you are
recovering, detachment can help you in many day-to-
day situations.

All too often we get consumed in the tensions, feelings,
thoughts, and actions of a moment. Like a small boat
tossed around in a large ocean we are exposed to a
million and one different irritants, aggravations, and

Practical DIY

Learning the art of detachment

There are many different situations when detachment can help you to make the best choices and to stay in the calmest frame of mind to see you through. Here is a range of ways in which you can practice detachment in everyday life.

♥ *Catch yourself getting caught up, make the decision to step back and let go of your attachment to the irritant.*

♥ *Visualize a barrier between you and the situation or thing aggravating you. Put on your armor.*

♥ *Put it into perspective. Ask yourself the following questions. Is this worth it? How much energy does this really warrant? Is this going to be important in two days, two weeks, two months, or two years? Then walk away and spend 5 minutes tuning in to your spirit. Visualize your spiritual flame perfectly still and untouched by the external struggles you are facing. Visualize the problem as a really small object in your hand and hold the object at arm's length.*

annoyances each and every day. By nurturing your strength of spirit as demonstrated in the exercises in Step 5 you can help ground and balance yourself through such conditions. By practicing the art of detachment you can step back from the daily chaos life brings, and anchor your boat so that all the unnecessary fuss and bother doesn't touch you.

When you are emotive, stressed, or overwhelmed by events you don't have a clear viewpoint. The moment that you want to make a decision, if you step back and move away from the problem not only do you get a better perspective on the situation, you fundamentally shift the energy surrounding the condition. Perspective enables us to see the situation with greater clarity and understanding, therefore enabling us to make better decisions and judgments.

Life is hard, challenging, and difficult. You can't be unrealistic and expect it to always be wonderful. What you can do is to prepare strategies for dealing with the difficult moments. Use detachment as a life skill and enjoy keeping your distance from all those annoying irritants so that your energy is directed where it's needed most: your heart. Use detachment to keep your life and its problems in perspective.

6. Personal responsibility

This is your life and every decision, action, and choice that you have made has brought you to where you are now—even if that's an uncomfortable thought in terms of your heartbreak, it is the truth. While blame culture is rampant in the litigious capitals of the world, the real crux of life is personal responsibility. We each have our own unique path to walk and no one else can share your path.

Practical DIY

Keeping your energy intact

By standing in a particular way you can close down the natural energy that flows around your body so that other people cannot draw upon it or influence it in any way. Done casually, no one will guess what you are doing! You have to be sitting or leaning against something that will take your full weight. Cross your ankles and either fold your arms across your solar plexus, or cup or hold your hands so that the thumbs and fingers of both hands are touching each other (alternatively, you can just connect your index fingers and thumbs).

You have free will: it is part and parcel of the gift of life. You must be in the driving seat and take responsibility for your heart, your life, and your journey. If you don't, you simply become an empty vessel tossed around carelessly by everyone else's choices. Your life becomes a consequence of everyone else's thoughts and actions. Loss of personal responsibility is loss of personal power.

Accept the challenge of personal responsibility and take your power back. It might not be easy and there are certain sacrifices to be made—you can't make excuses, point the finger of blame at other people, and announce it's their fault. But while the buck does stop with you, you will have the satisfaction of knowing that you, at least in your personal world, are your own boss.

Be accountable not just for your thoughts and actions but also for the influence that you have on others. The law of karma governs life on earth; it teaches us that we reap the consequences of all that we do, and inherent in this is the need to accept personal responsibility. Strive to do the best that you can, to be the best that you can, and you will be playing a constructive hand in your own karma. Be kind and compassionate, carry peace and love in your heart, and never know-ingly inflict suffering on others.

By taking ownership of your deeds and embracing per-sonal responsibility, you will place yourself in the best possible position to navigate this life. Your heart and your desire will be in your own hands, and you can decide where they're best placed at every step of the journey.

By working with the spiritual truths shared in Step 6 you can carry onward with your life and transform the pain of heartbreak into the wonder of personal trans-formation, fulfillment, and enlightenment. There is no end to the magic and potential that you can achieve now that you have opened the door of insight.

Conclusion
— ∎ —

*L*ife is an endless journey of learning that takes us across many different landscapes of experiences and events. As we travel along the pathway of life there will be times of great joy and happiness, as well as times of great sadness and pain. While it is possible to learn and evolve in moments that are happy and wonderful, life is often our best teacher when it delivers the cruelest blows. It is in these moments, when trauma shatters the foundations of your world and you find yourself stripped of all comfort and security, that the greatest opportunities of learning and discovery lie.

When beset with chaos many people become so consumed with the events taking place that they fail to see the lessons available to them. They get so tied up in the detail they cannot see the wood for the trees. What you have learned is that it is not so much *what* has taken place that counts but how you choose to respond to it.

Faced with heartache, you had the choice to curl up and give in to negativity and despair, or to make a commitment to your own healing and recovery. You chose to do something positive; you chose to be proactive in your healing and to mend your broken heart.

You might not yet have reached the point where you are 100 percent better, but you have achieved great things. You have turned a negative into a positive, and used your grief as a springboard for knowledge and personal development. You have thrown open the doors to learning and become a wiser, stronger, and richer person. You have delved in to the magnificence of your spiritual heart and tapped in to the fabulous resources that lie within. You have fanned the flame of your eternal spirit and opened the gateway to your higher consciousness and the universe.

In the days and weeks to come you will continue to grow and learn. There is always more that you can do to refine and cleanse as you delve deeper into the layers of life's experiences and its heartbreak.

Conclusion

Heartache can be viewed as a great teacher that knocks upon the door of man's understanding and awareness. It strengthens, refines and rounds the spirit, and gives greater stature and depth to the soul. As a result of the pain you have experienced you will always possess a greater understanding of love, and be able to offer true compassion and empathy to others.

As noted earlier in this book, it is often the most traumatic moments that prove to be the most significant turning points in life. In just the same way that the blackest part of the night precedes the first light of dawn you will discover that the darkest moments of your life can turn out to be your greatest triumphs. There will come a time, if not today then maybe later, when you will realize the reasons why this relationship had to take place and also why it had to end. You will find that understanding has replaced sadness, and that loss has given way to acceptance and insight. Instead of crying because it is over you will be able to smile because it happened.

Thanks to the work that you have done with the six steps presented here, you have freed yourself from the chains of bitterness and resentment. You have cleared the emotional baggage that could have ensnared your heart. This means that when love once again enters your world you will be free to give your love unconditionally. Enriched and wiser from your heartbreak you will be able to enter into your next relationship with a heart filled with a new sense of possibility, gratitude, and appreciation.

The power and potential that you have opened up knows no bounds, for the knowledge that you have accumulated from your heartbreak and throughout these six spiritual steps is timeless. You have found the stepping stones in your unique landscape of life and, day by day, step by step, you can move forward on your path of understanding and unfolding. The only limits that now exist are those that you set upon yourself.

Whether you realize it right now or you come to realize it in the days ahead, there will come a time when you know your heart has mended. You will become aware that not only is it whole again but that it is even larger, stronger, and more magnificent than before. The next person to enter into a relationship with you is going to be one very, very lucky person as you are now capable of giving even more abundant, deeper, and richer love than you thought possible

****

A message of hope and encouragement from the author

I hope that *Six Spiritual Steps to Mend a Broken Heart* has helped you to come to terms with your broken heart and has shown you the tools with which to mend its wounds. I hope that you have opened the door of curiosity to a world of new or extended beliefs, and that as you journey forward stronger and wiser for the experience of heartbreak, your spiritual self continues to shine and you continue to unfold in whatever way you choose.

I hope that what began as six spiritual steps has evolved into an amazing journey. You have taken hundreds of steps and traveled a vast distance. You should be proud of this and the achievements that you have made. I hope that, as you take a moment to reflect upon the road you have traveled, you can see an exciting future before you. I hope that the road that lies ahead of you is filled with laughter and happiness, that the universe lights your way, and that, one day, your stepping stones will lead you into the timeless fields of love and to the soul-mate that I firmly believe awaits each one of us.

Handy Hints for Using Crystals, Essential Oils, Creative Visualizations, and Flower Essences

— ∎ —

The information here is intended to be just a very basic introduction to help you get started and use these amazing tools. Further reading is highly recommended, and some useful books are listed in the appropriate sections. If you have any medical condition or are unsure about the suitability for you of any of the products mentioned, seek professional advice.

Crystals

BUYING A CRYSTAL

♥ Buy the crystal that has the properties that you require; alternatively, go for the crystals that you are immediately attracted to.

♥ Always look for crystals that are clear and
bright with a good natural color.
♥ Clean your crystals as soon as you bring
them home from the store.

HOW TO USE A CRYSTAL

You can hold your crystals or carry them in your
pocket, in a pouch, or even in a wallet. You can wear
them as jewelery. You can tape them to your body or
place them on yourself when you are lying down.
Crystals will emit their unique vibration of energy
wherever they are placed—they will still work under
your pillow, on the mantelpiece, by your bed, or on
your desk. Do not allow your crystals to become con-
taminated by other people handling them.

Crystals exert a subtle yet powerful energetic influence
on the body. Be aware of any sensations, thoughts,
images, or feelings that arise. The more you use them,
the more attuned with them you will become.

CLEANING YOUR CRYSTALS

It is important to clean your crystals regularly in order
to remove any residual, unwanted energies they have
absorbed, and to recharge them. Ask advice at the point

of sale about how to look after the particular crystals you have chosen.

Here are some general guidelines for cleansing and recharging your crystals.

- ♥ Incense or smudge sticks made of sage, sandalwood, frankincense or juniper clean and recharge crystals. Allow the smoke to pass around the crystal.
- ♥ Stand them in a bowl of sea salt for a day (throw the salt away afterwards).
- ♥ Hold a ringing bell or a vibrating tuning fork over the crystal.
- ♥ Leave the crystals in the sunlight or the moonlight to recharge them.

When experimenting with different crystals/stones be careful, as some dissolve in water while others chip and crack in heat.

For further information on crystals the following books are highly recommended:

The Crystal Bible, by Judy Hall (2003) Godsfield Press Ltd.

The Crystal Healing Pack, by Judy Hall (2005) Godsfield Press Ltd.

Crystals and Chakra Energies, by Sue and Simon Lily (2003/2004) Hermes House.

The Essential Crystal Handbook: All The Crystals You Will Ever Need for Health, Healing and Happiness, by Simon Lily (2006) Duncan Baird Publishers.

Essential oils

GENERAL SAFETY PRECAUTIONS WHEN USING ESSENTIAL OILS
Essential oils are very powerful and should be treated and used with great respect. Always check the suitability of the oil you wish to use with the manufacturer's guidelines, at the point of sale, or with a professional before using your chosen oil. Be aware of the contraindications that some oils can cause, especially if you are pregnant, have high or low blood pressure, have a medical condition, or are elderly. Here are some basic guidelines to get you started.

- ♥ Always read label cautions and warnings.
- ♥ Essential oils must never be ingested or taken orally. Keep all essential oils well out of the reach of children and pets.

♥ Avoid contact with the eyes. If oil does get into the eyes rinse with sweet almond oil and seek medical attention.

♥ Some essential oils can cause skin irritation if they are exposed to the sun; this includes ginger, lemon, orange, and bergamot. If you have sensitive skin use a 1 percent dilution (normal dilution is 2.5 percent) to prevent an allergic reaction.

MIXING WITH A CARRIER OIL

Only lavender and tea tree oil can be used directly on the skin. *All other essential oils* need to be mixed with a carrier oil such as sweet almond, grapeseed, sunflower, wheatgerm, or soy bean. Before deciding on a carrier oil make sure you complete the skin sensitivity test described below—you can be allergic and react to carrier oils just as much as the essential oils.

SKIN PATCH TEST

Put a drop of diluted oil on the gauze of a plaster and tape it to the soft skin on the inside of your wrist for 24 hours. Then check your skin for a reaction—if it is irritated, red, or sensitive do not use the blend; if the area appears clear you can use the oil.

HOW YOU CAN USE ESSENTIAL OILS

- ♥ **Anointing:** add 1–2 drops of essential oil to candles (blow out the candle, drop oil onto the wax then relight the candle) as well as crystals.

- ♥ **Bed:** add a few drops of your chosen essential oil to a piece of cotton and place in a bowl on the bedside table. You can sprinkle directly into the pillow case but some oils do stain.

- ♥ **Baths:** add 6–8 drops of essential oil(s) to your bath water.

- ♥ **Burners:** add 5–8 drops of essential oil blend to the top reservoir of an oil burner and heat with a tea light. Light bulb rings and electric diffusers are also available. Ensure water is kept topped up.

- ♥ **House:** add a few drops of your chosen essential oil to a charcoal block if you wish the scent to slowly diffuse through the house.

- ♥ **Spritzer:** add 5–8 drops of essential oil to 1 teaspoon of distilled water and put the mix in a small hand-held mister.

- ♥ **Misters:** 50–75 drops of essential oil can be added to a water spray mister filled with spring water.
- ♥ **Massage:** add 5 drops of essential oils to 1 tablespoon of oil.

For further information on essential oils the following books are highly recommended:

Aromatherapy for Common Ailments, by Shirley Price (2004) Simon and Schuster Inc.

Aromatherapy for Healing the Spirit: Restoring Emotional and Mental Balance with Essential Oils, by Gabriel Mojay (2005) Gaia Books Ltd.

The Complete Guide to Aromatherapy, by Salvatore Battaglia (2004) Perfect Potion.

Creative visualizations

Creative visualization is the art of producing pictures in the mind's eye. If you have never attempted a creative visualization before try this—close your eyes right now and picture a rosy red apple. Easy isn't it! And, like most things, the more you practice the better the clarity, color, and quality of image you will be able to picture.

As a beginner there are some simple guidelines that can help you.

♥ Find somewhere where you can be alone and won't be disturbed or interrupted (turn your phone off!). You can stand or sit, but it is important to be comfortable.

♥ Close your eyes and begin with a few gentle breathing exercises. This will help you to still your brain and enable you to connect to your own spiritual center. Breathing also draws energy into your being and opens your higher consciousness.

♥ When you are ready, begin the visualization that you have chosen, run it through your mind's eye as if it were a movie playing inside your head. Do not worry if it is in black and white or color. Do not worry if thoughts pop into your mind or you drift off from the visualization, just go back to it and continue where you left off.

♥ When you have finished the visualization give yourself a few moments to collect your thoughts and reorient yourself.

Some people find creative visualizations very easy, others need to put in a little more effort and practice to get the hang of them. They can take anywhere between a few minutes and 50 minutes, depending on how much time you have available.

Enjoy following your intuition with the creative visualizations on offer. Feel free to adapt them in whatever way you sense, feel, know, or think is right for you. Repeat the exercise frequently to enjoy the full benefits and do not be surprised if the most amazing and unexpected changes take place!

With time you will be able to do creative visualizations with great ease. You will even be able to do them with your eyes open, surrounded by people and noise. You will find you can sustain the image for increasing periods of time without any intrusion from your mind, and the clarity of what you are visualizing will improve dramatically.

For further information on creative visualizations the following book is highly recommended:

Creative Visualisation, by Shakti Gawain (2002) New World Library.

Flower remedies

Flower remedies are the homeopathically prepared essences of non-poisonous flowers, plants, bushes, and trees. The picked flower or plant is placed in spring water and heated by sunlight (in some cases they are also boiled). In this way the healing essence—the unique vibration of the plant's or flower's energy—is transferred into the water and, when taken orally, passes into the body.

Safe, non-toxic, and non-addictive, flower remedies can be taken by anyone. They can be used in conjunction with any other alterative or conventional medicine with no fear of contraindications. They are not therapeutic drugs, instead they work on the mind, body, and soul to bring about harmony and health. Acting as catalysts, flower remedies help to resolve a diverse range of negative emotional and mental states.

USING FLOWER REMEDIES

♥ Take 3–4 drops under the tongue three times a day. The drops can be diluted into water, milk, or juice. Take them 10 minutes before a meal and an hour after eating. When you go to bed and when you get up in the morning are especially important times to take the drops.

♥ You can increase the dosage to between 10 and 20 drops a day.

♥ You can combine a maximum of seven flower remedies. To do so add two drops of each essence to two tablespoons of spring water. Store the liquid solution in a dark brown or blue bottle. A teaspoon of brandy or cider vinegar can be added as a preservative.

♥ 16 drops of flower remedies can be added to bath water.

♥ Flower remedies can also be added to lotions, creams, and oils.

For further information on flower remedies the following books are highly recommended:

Bach Flower Remedies for Women, by Judy Howard (2005) Vermilion.

The Bach Flower Remedies Step by Step: A Complete Guide to Selecting and Using the Remedies, by Judy Howard (2005) Vermilion.

Bloom: Using Flower Essences for Personal Development and Spiritual Growth, by Stefan Ball (2006) Vermilion.

Fiona Hickman-Taylor is a writer and clairvoyant medium who, over the past sixteen years, has transformed people's lives with her unique blend of spiritual counselling, philosophy, clairvoyance and Neuro Linguistic Programming (NLP). Having lectured for ten years in art and design, she now runs an interior design company that specializes in inspired and imaginative interiors.

Fiona can be contacted at *fiona@the-soul-doctor.co.uk*